Praise for *ISRAEL MATTERS*

"In *Israel Matters*, Mitchell Bard offers a comprehensive yet handy text that gives readers a practical understanding of the State of Israel—its historical importance, and its relevance today. Bard provides a noble service for readers who want to connect with and learn about a nation-state that has changed the world."

— SENATOR JOE LIEBERMAN

"Without ignoring some of the controversial aspects of life in modern Israel, *Israel Matters* conveys the broad scope of Israeli history and culture in an engaging and accessible manner. The mini-biographies of everyday Israelis and the sections entitled "What Would YOU Do?" are particularly helpful in connecting young readers with the context and moral dilemmas of daily life in the Jewish state. *Israel Matters* very successfully addresses the long-recognized need for a text that presents contemporary Israel to American youth."

— DR. ROBERT WEXLER, PRESIDENT, AMERICAN JEWISH UNIVERSITY

"Israel does matter, but how little we really know about its history, current challenges, and how to find our way about it. This extraordinarily readable and valuable book by Mitchell Bard—an outstanding expert on all these topics—is just what is needed."

— ILAN TROEN, DIRECTOR, SCHUSTERMAN CENTER FOR ISRAEL STUDIES, BRANDEIS UNIVERSITY

"Instead of the cardboard cutout descriptions of Israel one reads either in the popular media or promotional literature, Mitchell Bard presents a three-dimensional Israel— full of political debate, cultural clash, and the human dilemmas of real people."

— ROBERT SATLOFF, EXECUTIVE DIRECTOR, THE WASHINGTON INSTITUTE FOR NEAR EAST POLICY

"Lively, substantive, accessible."

—DR. GIL TROY, PROFESSOR OF HISTORY, McGILL UNIVERSITY

ISRAEL MATTERS

Understand the Past
Look to the Future

Mitchell Bard

BEHRMAN HOUSE
www.behrmanhouse.com

Originally published by the Jewish Federation of Greater Los Angeles
Managing Editor: Marla Markman
Developmental Editor: Tammy Ditmore
Design and Composition: Eliot House Productions

Revised edition published by Behrman House, Inc.
Springfield, New Jersey 07081
www.behrmanhouse.com
ISBN 978-0-87441-858-3

Project Manager: Dena Neusner
Designer: Annemarie Redmond

Library of Congress Cataloging-in-Publication Data

Bard, Mitchell Geoffrey, 1959-
 Israel matters : understand the past, look to the future / By Mitchell Bard.
    p. cm.
 "Originally published by The Jewish Federation of Greater Los Angeles."
 Includes bibliographical references and index.
 ISBN 978-0-87441-858-3 (alk. paper)
 1. Israel—Juvenile literature. 2. Israel. I. Title.
 DS126.5.B2636 2012
 956.94—dc23   2011052123
 Printed in the United States of America

Visit www.behrmanhouse.com/israel-matters for more Israel resources.

To my children, Ariel and Daniel, and their generation,
which will be entrusted with securing Israel's future

In loving memory of Paul Tashman

With deep gratitude to Dr. Daniel Lieber

ACKNOWLEDGMENTS

I would especially like to thank my assistants, Jennifer Feinberg and Yariv Nornberg, for their input and contributions to the manuscript. I would also like to express my appreciation to the following people for their comments and suggestions: William Gutterman, Jill Kulekofsky Selman, Dr. David Lieber, Dr. Daniel Lieber, Elaine Albert, Rabbi Hal Greenwald, and Dr. David Ackerman. Thank you to those who commented on the new edition: Rabbi William Cutter, Irwin Field, John Fitzsimons, Lesley Litman, and Dr. Gil Troy. Please note that the views in this book do not necessarily reflect the views of the scholars who read and contributed to it. I would also like to thank Tammy Ditmore for editing the book and the extraordinary effort she made to convert my research into a more readable text for students.

TABLE OF CONTENTS

INTRODUCTION

Israel is frequently mentioned in newspaper headlines and on the Internet. Commentators often debate its policies, its politics, and its conflicts. Perhaps you know about Israel from school or from your knowledge of the Bible, or from discussions with friends and family, or from the media. If you have visited Israel, or have Israeli relatives or friends, you may have a different perspective about the country than your peers, who have formed their impressions primarily from news sources.

The idea of Israel as the Jewish homeland may feel like an abstract concept to many American Jews. You may be someone who already has a personal connection to Israel, or you may be less familiar with the Jewish state. And without a direct relationship, it can be challenging to feel a sense of connection. After all: Israel is a country on the other side of the world that you are told you *should* care about, but you may not know *why* you should care. If you ever attended a Jewish school, you probably learned "Hatikvah," Israel's national anthem, just as you learned "The Star-Spangled Banner." But what is behind the singing of "Hatikvah"? Do you feel a sense of patriotism toward Israel because you are Jewish? Maybe. Maybe not.

Many Jews call themselves Zionists. For some this means they believe all Jews should live in Israel. Others believe they can be Zionists and support Israel in their own way from their homes in the United States, Canada, the United Kingdom, or elsewhere around the world. Some Christians also consider themselves Zionists and believe in supporting a Jewish homeland. Others support Israel in their own way, but choose not to call themselves Zionists. You may resist the idea of any label and prefer to figure out what, if any, relationship you want to have with this small country.

When most people talk about Israel, they talk about the pressing issues of the moment. Yet it is impossible to understand the context of the issues without looking at *all* the dimensions of this small country: its historical and religious significance, its technological achievements, and its archaeological wonders. One needs to understand the remarkable diversity of its population and the countless personal stories that shape its culture. And one needs to appreciate Israel's beautiful beaches, scenic deserts, and geological wonders. Not to mention its great cuisine, exciting nightlife, and influential arts scene.

Often discussions about Israel focus on controversial issues: the hardships of the Palestinians, Israel's internal social problems, and secular-religious conflicts. When you hear criticism of Israel, what do you think? Do you know whether the criticism is accurate or not? Do you try to find out? Do you feel compelled to respond? Not everyone likes to argue or debate, but you may still want to find out the answers for yourself to make your own judgments. Or maybe you do feel the need to correct misinformation and advocate on Israel's behalf, based on *your* understanding of the issues. Either way, the answers to these difficult questions often are not black or white, but are more complicated.

This book was written to help you sort out these complex questions and help you form your own relationship to Israel. It offers one perspective in what should be a toolbox of materials that help you examine Israel from a variety of historical, political, and cultural perspectives. It is a place to begin the conversation.

I hope that you will read this book and come away with a basic understanding of Israel's history, politics, and culture, and some of the dilemmas its people face. I hope it helps you discover how Israel matters to you. And I hope you will feel confident enough in your knowledge of the topic to participate in discussions about Israel and help others discover that Israel matters to them as well.

CHAPTER ONE

A VIBRANT COUNTRY

Israel. The very name may bring to mind images of ancient kings or modern-day battles. But the story of Israel extends far beyond picture-book tales or news reports of conflict between neighbors. Contemporary Israel is a vibrant country that is dense with archaeological sites and other reminders of its ancestral history. Israel is a country where names of cities and towns evoke memories of biblical times even as its residents participate in a modern culture of dance, music, sports, and drama. Israel is a tiny country with a sophisticated high-tech sector and major research universities, and a young democracy that has survived and thrived against almost impossible odds.

Israel is also a physically beautiful country that features a diversity of environments, even though the whole nation is only eight thousand square miles in area. On Israel's west coast, along the Mediterranean, you can find some of the world's most beautiful beaches; go south to Eilat for spectacular scuba diving in the Red Sea. Also in the south are rocky and scenic deserts. Head north to ski on Mount Hermon in the winter. At Rosh Hanikrah, in the northeastern corner, ride a cable car down to sea level to breathtaking white cliffs and grottoes. In the middle of the country, you can float effortlessly in the Dead Sea, the lowest

Faces of Israel

Udi, eighteen, lives in Tel Aviv. On his iPod, he listens to the Red Hot Chili Peppers sing about the California surf as he lies on his bed staring up at the ceiling. In two weeks he will take the *bagrut*, the achievement test he needs to pass to get into college. And in five weeks he will go with all his friends into the induction center for army orientation. After orientation, Udi will spend the next three years in uniform, when all he really wants to do is grab his surfboard and ride. But he can't forget that he once made a pledge to his best friend, Shai, promising that he would try out for the elite paratrooper unit.

The music of Hadag Nahash, Udi's favorite Israeli hip-hop group, pops up next on his playlist, and he cranks up the volume: "Bombs, pressure, crooked politicians / When will it end? Who knows? / But that's your buddy over there / and that's your black hat wacked cousin in the Holy Crazy City / and there's nowhere else you'd rather be than right here in the middle of the *balagan* [chaos]."

point on earth, where the salt content of the water is so high that you can't help bobbing on the surface.

Israel is dense with forests and parks. Since the late nineteenth century, the planting of trees in the Land of Israel has been a national priority. In fact, Israel is the only country to end the twentieth century with more trees than it had when the century started.

LIVING HISTORY
Ancient Ruins and Modern Museums

The long, rich history of Israel comes alive in archaeological parks and museums. When you visit, you will find many well-preserved Roman ruins, such as the amphitheater used today for performances in Caesarea. Or you can explore excavations of even older civilizations, such as the Nabateans, who lived in the Negev desert, and ancient sites like the five-thousand-year-old city of Megiddo, which is referred to as Armageddon in the New Testament. One of the most spectacular sites is Masada, a fortress where a group of Jews known as Zealots made a three-year stand against the Romans; in the end they took their own lives rather than surrender.

Visitors from all over the world come to Israeli museums to view and study their showcases of ancient artifacts. The most famous of these is the Dead Sea Scrolls, which are housed in their own special section, known as the Shrine of the Book, at the Israel Museum in Jerusalem. The scrolls, discovered between 1947 and 1956 in desert caves near the Dead Sea, contain the oldest known copies of parts of the Hebrew Bible.

California
158,302 sq. mi.

New Jersey
8,729 sq. mi.

Israel is a small country, consisting of only 8,522 square miles. Compare the size of Israel to the states of California and New Jersey.

Look Closer

When referencing dates, many scholars now use the terms "before the Common Era," abbreviated BCE, and "of the Common Era," abbreviated CE. These replace the markers you may be more used to seeing, BC—"before Christ"—and AD—*anno Domini*, which in Latin means "in the year of the Lord." BCE and CE are seen as being more neutral terms.

At Beit Hatfutsot (the Museum of the Jewish People) in Tel Aviv, you can learn about the history of the worldwide Jewish community. Other museums around the country display Islamic art, scientific exhibits, and contemporary sculpture.

Landmarks of Faith

The Land of Israel is home to three of the world's major religions; shrines important to the Jewish, Christian, and Islamic faiths are found throughout the country. Many are located in the Old City of Jerusalem, and several are centered around the Temple Mount, an area of roughly thirty-seven acres on which the Jewish Temple was built around 950 BCE. At the Western Wall you can visit the last remains of the retaining wall of the Temple Mount. The Mount is the holiest site in Judaism and the Western Wall has been the place where Jews have prayed for generations. The city of Jerusalem has been the object of Jewish respect, admiration, and prayer since the Second Temple was destroyed in 70 CE.

If you visit the Western Wall, you will notice the adjoining Dome of the Rock, famous for its blue tile walls and glittering gold dome, and the Al-Aqsa Mosque, built hundreds of years after the Romans destroyed the Second Temple. Islam teaches that Muhammad ascended to heaven from this spot; Muslims count it as their third most holy site, after Mecca and Medina.

Not far away, amid narrow streets filled with small shops selling trinkets, food, and souvenirs, you can walk the Via Dolorosa. This is the route Christians believe Jesus walked as he carried the cross on the way to his Crucifixion. You can also visit the Church of the Holy Sepulchre, which most Christians believe

Look Closer

While many Americans head to college after high school, most Israelis graduate from high school and begin military service. Men are required to serve for thirty-six months and women for twenty-one months in the Israel Defense Forces (IDF), which is made up of the army, air force, and navy. Although most Israeli Jews must serve in the military, some perform community service instead, and certain categories of people are exempt, including many ultra-Orthodox (*Haredi*) Jews, who are allowed to study in *yeshivot,* religious schools. This is a controversial issue that is often debated by Israelis.

Israeli women have been fighting in combat units since 1994 and currently are eligible to serve in most IDF positions. The first female fighter pilot received her wings in 2001.

Following regular military service, men may be called for reserve duty of up to one month annually until they are forty-three to forty-five years old (many volunteer to serve as long as they are physically fit) and may be called for active duty in times of crisis. Most of Israel's army is made up of reserves, so when an emergency occurs, thousands of Israelis leave their jobs and their homes to join their units.

The IDF takes great pride in what it calls the "purity of arms"—the commitment to avoid inflicting unnecessary injury to prisoners of war and civilians.

was built on the site where Jesus was crucified. The church is thought to be the place where Jesus was buried (the sepulchre), and it has been an important pilgrimage destination since at least the fourth century.

Many other religions have a presence in Israel, including the Baha'i, a small faith whose world headquarters in Haifa features a gold-domed shrine that overlooks spectacular gardens on a hillside above the Mediterranean Sea.

> " My favorite destination in Israel is Jerusalem. It was the first place where I felt most connected. I think I got butterflies in my stomach and my face was beaming when we emerged out of the tunnel and I had my first glimpse of the city. "
>
> ELISSA, AGE 26,
> NEW YORK, NEW YORK

LIVELY CULTURE

Israel is home to a thriving cultural and arts scene, which began to develop even before Israel became an independent nation in 1948. Hayyim Nahman Bialik was a famous poet who lived in the early twentieth century, and Shmuel Yosef Agnon was a famous writer who in 1966 became the only Israeli so far to win the Nobel Prize in Literature. Other Israeli writers and poets have developed international reputations, including Yehuda Amichai, Nathan Alterman, David Grossman, A. B. Yehoshua, Shulamith Hareven, and Amos Oz.

The Israeli Philharmonic Orchestra was founded in 1936, and the country's premier art school, the Bezalel Academy of Arts and Design, was created even earlier, in 1906. HaBima Theater opened in Tel Aviv in 1931, and popular playwrights such as Hanoch Levin, Yehoshua Sobol, and Shmuel Hasfari have become well-known in recent years. Folk dancing was popular before Israel's independence, and renowned contemporary dance companies, such as Batsheva and Bat-Dor, have popularized modern dance and ballet.

Israel has produced some of the world's most famous classical musicians, including violinists Itzhak Perlman and Pinchas Zukerman, and Argentina-born pianist and conductor Daniel Barenboim. The arrival of thousands of immigrants from the former Soviet Union in the 1980s and 1990s also brought many extraordinary musicians who helped establish new orchestras, chamber music groups, and choirs. In addition to classical music, Israel is known for its popular performing artists, such as Arik Einstein and David Broza. More and more young Israelis listen to hip-hop and rap, and groups such as Subliminal, Hadag Nahash, and Muki have gained international followings. Singers such as Chava Alberstein and Noa have also spread Jewish music to the whole world.

Have You Heard of Hayyim Nahman Bialik? (1873-1934)

Born in Russia to a traditional Jewish family, Bialik studied at the great Talmudic academy in Volozhin, Lithuania, but he gradually drifted away from religion. Bialik's first published poem was "El Ha-Tzipor" ("To the Bird"), and in 1901 his first collection of poems, all in Hebrew, appeared to critical acclaim. Bialik moved to Berlin in 1921, where he founded the Dvir publishing house.

In 1924, he moved the company to Tel Aviv, where he devoted himself to cultural activities and public affairs. He became head of the Hebrew Writers Union in 1927 and retained this position until his death in 1934. During his lifetime, he was called Israel's "national poet." His poems are still popular and have been set to music by several of Israel's most gifted composers.

Israel also has a very active film and television industry that has gained increasing international recognition as a result of award-winning and sometimes controversial films, such as *Walk on Water* (2004), *The Band's Visit* (2007), *Waltz with Bashir* (2008), and *Ajami* (2009). One of Israel's popular TV shows, *BeTipul,* was the basis for the HBO series *In Treatment.* And Israeli-born actors, such as Natalie Portman, have become international movie and television stars.

Israel has outstanding art museums renowned for their significant collections of work by Jewish artists, such as Marc Chagall. And Israeli craftspeople are known for their ceramics, jewelry, glass blowing, and calligraphy. You can

Have You Heard of Itzhak Perlman? (1945–)

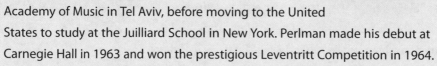

Born in Tel Aviv just a few years before Israel formally became a country, concert violinist Itzhak Perlman contracted polio at the age of four and has needed crutches to walk ever since. He began playing the violin as a child and studied at the Academy of Music in Tel Aviv, before moving to the United States to study at the Juilliard School in New York. Perlman made his debut at Carnegie Hall in 1963 and won the prestigious Leventritt Competition in 1964.

Perlman is regarded as one of the world's greatest violinists, with an extensive recording career and appearances all over the world. He has performed several times at the White House and made guest appearances on US television shows. You might have seen him when he performed at President Barack Obama's 2009 inauguration.

Have You Heard of Natalie Portman? (1981-)

You may recognize Natalie Hershlag by her stage name, Natalie Portman, or perhaps you know her from one of her many movie roles, such as Queen Amidala from the *Star Wars* prequel trilogy. Natalie was born in Jerusalem, and her family moved to the United States when she was three. At ten, Portman started to act at theater camps. She landed her first movie role two years later in *The Professional*. Still in her teens, Portman performed in a series of movies, made her Broadway debut as Anne Frank in *The Diary of Anne Frank,* and then rocketed to fame when she landed the role of Queen Amidala.

Portman graduated with honors from Syosset High School on Long Island, New York, and went on to major in psychology at Harvard. During school breaks, she filmed *Cold Mountain* and *Garden State*. Her 2005 film, *Free Zone*, was directed by Israeli Amos Gitai and shot in Israel and Jordan. In 2010, she won the Academy Award for Actress in a Leading Role for her performance in *Black Swan*.

In addition to her film career, Portman has served as the Ambassador of Hope with the Foundation for International Community Assistance, an organization that provides small loans to women in Third World countries so they can start their own businesses. She lives in New York and speaks Hebrew fluently.

buy beautiful works of art in artists' colonies throughout the country, including the city of Jaffa and the Arab market in the Old City of Jerusalem.

Just like millions of people all over the world, Israelis are passionate about sports. If you lived in Israel, you would probably watch soccer and basketball and be proud because Israel has become a basketball powerhouse, winning the European championship five times (and coming in second place nine times). Maccabi Tel Aviv is the country's most famous team.

Israelis also excel in other sports, and, in 1992, Israel won its first Olympic medals when Yael Arad took a silver and Oren Smadja a bronze in judo. In 2004, windsurfer Gal Friedman won Israel's first Olympic gold medal.

THRIVING ECONOMY

Remarkably, in just over six decades, Israel has achieved significant economic growth and developed a large high-tech sector and an advanced agricultural industry.

Agricultural Advances

When Jewish settlers arrived in the region at the end of the nineteenth and early twentieth centuries with dreams of creating a country, the land was largely barren; much of the area was infertile, and malarial swamps had to be drained. As farmers found ways to irrigate crops with scarce water supplies, they learned how to produce oranges and other fruits. Today, Israel not only grows enough food to feed its people but also exports many fruits, vegetables, flowers, and wines across the region and throughout Europe and even to the United States.

> " Israel has introduced this world to a great number of things we take for granted today. It's so awe-inspiring that such a small country can have such a technologically profound impact on things like medicine and communication. "
>
> BENJAMIN, AGE 17,
> ROCKVILLE, MARYLAND

Israeli researchers have also developed new ways to protect crops and animals from pests and diseases without the use of damaging pesticides. They devised techniques to improve dairy cow productivity, plant fertilization, tomato crop yields, wheat production, and farm efficiency. Israeli farmers benefit from these innovations and also share them with farmers in the United States and other countries. One well-known technique developed in Israel is

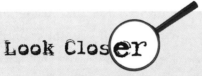

Look Closer

Israel is active in the development of innovative ways to use water more efficiently and prevent future water shortages. Israel's three main water sources, the coastal and mountain aquifers and Lake Kinneret (the Sea of Galilee), each supply approximately 25 percent of the total water consumed in Israel, with the remainder drawn from smaller aquifers and recycled sewage. Because Israel is subject to frequent droughts, the supply is not reliable.

As Israel's population grows and its economy expands, so does its need for water, which is used for agriculture, business, recreation, and drinking. Israel addresses its need for water preservation through the use of desalination, a process that removes salt from seawater, making the water suitable for drinking, washing, and agricultural purposes.

Israel is engaged in a major water development project and is in the process of building five desalination plants along the Mediterranean coast. In 2010, the world's largest desalination plant of its kind was opened in Hadera. However, most experts believe that while desalination can reduce Israel's water problems, it won't completely solve them. The plants are expensive, take a long time to build, use a lot of energy, and will not supply as much water as Israel will need in the future. Others worry that the plants will make tempting targets for terrorists. Despite the drawbacks, the technology is in high demand around the world, and Israel is hoping to become a leader in the global water technology market.

Look Closer

Because it has done so much with so little, Israel has become a model for other developing nations. From the early days of statehood, Israel has assisted other countries by sharing its experience and knowledge in agriculture, medicine, and sustainable development. Golda Meir, years before she became prime minister in 1969, initiated an assistance program for Africa because she believed many countries on that continent faced similar challenges and that Israel could provide help in overcoming them.

drip irrigation, which directs just the right amount of water to where it is most needed; this method is now used worldwide to improve agricultural yields.

High-Tech Giant

Despite economic challenges, Israel today has become renowned for its technological prowess. Given its small size, the country has produced a significant number of scientists and researchers. These talented individuals have created products and services that put Israel at the forefront of the telecommunications, computer, optics, and high-tech industries. Because of Israel's reputation for technological innovation, most of America's high-tech giants, such as Motorola, IBM, Microsoft, and Intel, have built facilities in Israel.

Israel has also advanced in many scientific fields beyond the computer industry. Israeli scientists are recognized as pioneers in fields such as medical research, where they have developed new drugs and treatments for a variety of illnesses, including multiple sclerosis and AIDS. An Israeli company developed a camera small enough to fit inside a pill; patients swallow the pill so doctors can view their small intestines to check for signs of cancer or other digestive disorders.

Another Israeli company has developed a device that could help millions of diabetics inject themselves with insulin—pain-free. In 2004, Israeli

Think about It

How did Israel achieve its successes in such a short period of time?

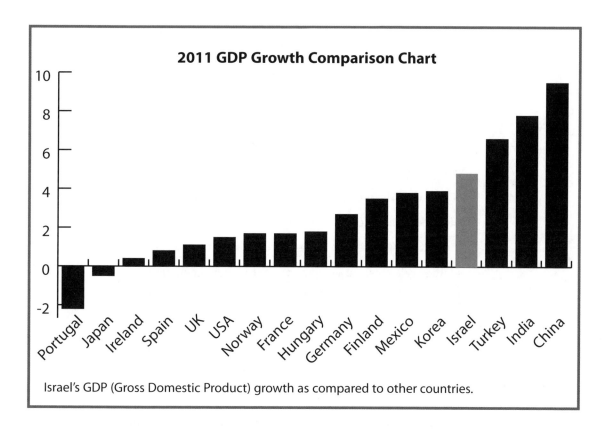

2011 GDP Growth Comparison Chart

Israel's GDP (Gross Domestic Product) growth as compared to other countries.

scientists Avram Hershko and Aaron Ciechanover won the Nobel Prize in Chemistry for groundbreaking work in cancer research, and in 2011, Israeli scientist Dan Shechtman won the Nobel Prize in Chemistry for a discovery in crystallography. Many outstanding hospitals can be found in Israel; Hadassah Hospital in Jerusalem, a world-class center for medical research and treatment, is known for its multiethnic staff and willingness to treat any patient, including both victims and perpetrators of terror.

The United States and Israel collaborate on many projects. Binational foundations, for

Word Work

wadi In Israel, a valley in the desert is called a *wadi*. Because Israel now has the largest concentration of high-tech companies outside of California's Silicon Valley, it is sometimes called the Silicon Wadi.

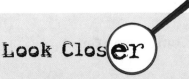

Look Closer

Many high-tech innovations were developed in Israel. Here are examples of just a few:

➪ Voice-over internet protocol (VoIP) technology

➪ Voice-mail technology

➪ AOL Instant Messenger technology

➪ Intel's new multi-core processor

➪ The first flight system to protect aircraft against missile attacks

➪ A large-scale solar-powered and fully functional electricity-generating plant launched in Southern California's Mojave Desert

➪ The first PC antivirus software

➪ A program that enabled NASA to transmit images from Mars

example, support joint development of commercial high-tech products, cooperative agricultural research, and collaborative projects in science, engineering, and social sciences. Almost every US government agency collaborates with an Israeli counterpart in fields ranging from education to energy to environmental protection. In addition, nearly half the individual US states have separate agreements to cooperate with Israel in areas such as trade and tourism.

Israelis experienced a surge of national pride in 2003 when Ilan Ramon became Israel's first astronaut to fly into space on NASA's shuttle. Their pride turned to grief when Ramon died along with all others aboard the *Columbia* as it broke apart upon its return to earth. Ramon was a national hero and a symbol of hope. His accomplishment remains a source of inspiration for Israelis, proving that this tiny country with ancient roots is ready to fly in the world of the twenty-first century.

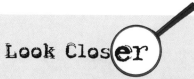

Look Closer

Before his shuttle flight, Ilan Ramon said he felt he was representing all Jews and all Israelis. Though he wasn't an observant Jew, special kosher meals were made for his journey, and he consulted with rabbis about the proper way to observe the Sabbath from space. Ramon carried a credit card-sized microfiche copy of the Bible and a pencil drawing titled "Moon Landscape" by a fourteen-year-old Jewish boy, Peter Ginz, who was killed at Auschwitz.

While orbiting the earth, Ilan Ramon shot a video of Israel from space. To view this online, go to www.factsofisrael.com/blog/archives/000617.html.

View of Israel and the Middle East from space.

Have You Heard of Shulamit Levenberg? (1969-)

Dr. Shulamit Levenberg, a biomedical engineer at the Technion, Israel's famous institute of technology in Haifa, was named one of the world's top fifty scientists by *Scientific American* in 2006. The magazine honored Professor Levenberg for her work in creating lab-manufactured tissues and organs for transplant with the hope of one day creating synthetic organs.

CHAPTER TWO

JEWISH LAND, JEWISH NATION

In just over sixty years this tiny country, populated by diverse immigrant groups, located in an arid region, and surrounded by enemies, has developed one of the strongest economies and most democratic governments in the region. To understand and appreciate Israel's current success and strength, you must look to its history.

CREATING A NATION

Although the modern nation of Israel was born in 1948, the Jewish connection to the land in what we today call the Middle East is ancient, dating to the biblical period. Jewish tradition teaches that some 3,700 years ago God made a special promise (or Covenant) to Abraham. The Hebrew Bible states that Abraham's descendants would inherit a land of milk and honey and that they would be as numerous as the stars in the heavens—if they followed God's commandments. According to the Hebrew Bible, that Covenant was fulfilled when the Israelites, the ancient Jews, followed Moses out of Egypt and created an independent nation in the region they called the Promised Land. Historical and archaeological records show that Jews can trace their lineage in this area to roughly the year 1000 BCE.

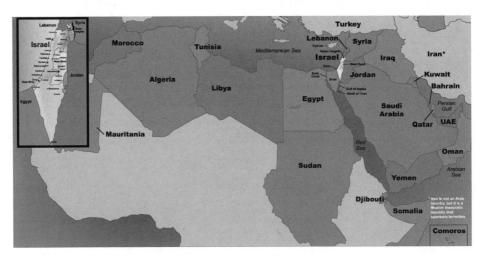

This map shows comparative sizes of Israel and its Arab neighbors.

According to biblical accounts, the twelve Jewish tribes that emerged from slavery in Egypt eventually united to form one of the world's first constitutional monarchies, which was ruled by Kings Saul, David, and Solomon. Because Israel is located at a crossroads between Asia and Africa, it is the site of valuable trade routes and has been a battleground for competing powers for centuries. The ruling kings built a dynasty that protected the twelve tribes from invasion and other threats. Ancient Israel, at its largest, included some or all of the modern-day countries of Israel, Syria, Lebanon, and Jordan.

But internal divisions led to a split in the Jewish nation. After Solomon's death around 922 BCE, ten of the twelve Israelite tribes broke away to form a new kingdom in the north that they called Israel. The remaining tribes stayed in the southern part of the original kingdom of Saul, David, and Solomon, and called their land Judah. Not surprisingly, the divided nation was much weaker, making the smaller kingdoms ripe targets for leaders from nearby countries who were seeking to expand their own rule.

Faces of Israel

Avraham, seventeen, was born in Jerusalem to a family of eleven children. His father is a well-respected rabbi, of the eleventh generation in his family to be ordained in Jerusalem. His mother takes care of the family and is involved with charitable activities within their community.

Avraham wakes up at 5:00 a.m. to begin his day at rabbinical school. He learns Jewish philosophy, rabbinic texts, and prayer. His favorite day of the week is the Sabbath, his day off from school. His extended family and their visiting guests gather for a festive meal that lasts for hours.

Avraham is looking forward to starting his own family in the next few years with a wife his parents will help him choose from within the community.

INDEPENDENCE LOST

After two centuries of independence, the northern kingdom of Israel was conquered by the Assyrians in 732 BCE. The southern kingdom of Judah held out for over three hundred years but was overwhelmed by the Babylonians in 586 BCE. Eventually the Babylonians were conquered by the Persians, who were in turn overrun by Alexander the Great and the Greeks. Still, the Jewish people never gave up their hope of regaining their independence. In 167 BCE, the Jews revolted against the Greek despot Antiochus under the courageous leadership of Mattathias and his five sons, who are known as the Maccabees. After three years of fighting, the Maccabees recaptured Jerusalem and rededicated the holy Temple, a story Jews around the world recall each year during the holiday of Hanukkah. An independent Jewish kingdom was restored in 142 BCE, after the Jewish people had lived for more than five hundred years under the rule of foreign powers. But this Jewish kingdom survived less than eighty years before succumbing to the Romans.

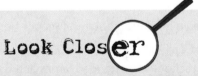

Look Closer

The family of Mattathias became known as the Maccabees, from the Hebrew word for "hammer," because they were said to strike hammer blows against their enemies. The family is more commonly known as the Hasmoneans, and their story is the basis of the Jewish holiday of Hanukkah.

Fighting the Romans

After the Romans conquered the Jewish Hasmonean kingdom, the Jewish population was determined to fight for freedom. In 66 CE, the Jews, led by a group called the Zealots, mounted a revolt that took Rome four years to put down. But the revolt cost the lives of perhaps one million Jews. Ultimately, after a long and bloody siege, the Romans breached the walls of Jerusalem in the summer of 70 CE and razed the Jewish Temple. This act was seen as the most devastating Roman blow yet against the Jewish people because of the Temple's religious significance and also because it represented the total loss of Jewish political authority in the region.

In 132 CE, Shimon Bar Kochba led yet another revolt against Roman rule that lasted almost three years. But by the time Rome put down this last rebellion, an estimated 50 percent of the Jewish population in the area had been killed, and the majority of Jews who survived were driven into exile by the Romans, who ruled the land of Israel for nearly eight centuries.

When you hear people today say that the Jewish people were homeless for two thousand years, they mean they had no country from the time the Temple was destroyed in 70 CE until the establishment of the State of Israel in 1948. However, even though most Jews were exiled by the Romans, there always has been a Jewish presence in the region.

Word Work

Zealot *Zealot* is a word that comes from the Greek meaning "enthusiastic." This term refers to one who exhibits great enthusiasm and dedication to a cause. In Jewish history, Zealots were a group that fought bitterly for Jewish independence from the Roman Empire.

> " Climbing Masada was inspiring. I not only witnessed a view but also an ancient civilization. I witnessed the way of life of my ancestors, and I empathized with their struggle to hold on to their values, and their lives. In my mind, this experience was yet another example of the necessity of Israel's safety and security. "
>
> ALLISON, AGE 17, ROCKVILLE, MARYLAND

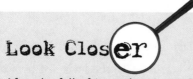

After the fall of Jerusalem in 70 CE, a group of Zealots fled Jerusalem to the fortress of Masada near the Dead Sea, where they resisted the Romans for three years. Once it became apparent the Romans would overrun their defenses, the leader of the group, Elazar ben Yair, decided it would be better for all of the remaining 960 Jews to take their own lives rather than be captured and sold as slaves. Though Judaism does not condone taking one's life, Masada has remained a powerful symbol to this day and is a popular destination of Jewish tourists visiting Israel.

Surviving after Defeat

Though what is known as the Great Revolt (66-70 CE) was a disaster for the Jewish people, one important development helped the Jews survive without a central religious or political center in the centuries to come. During the Roman siege of Jerusalem, one of the leading Jewish teachers, Rabbi Yochanan ben Zakkai, foresaw that the battle would be lost. He feared that if the Jewish people could no longer access the Temple or Jerusalem, they would no longer have a way to perpetuate their faith or govern themselves. He realized that the Jewish people needed an academy devoted to educating future generations.

But Rabbi ben Zakkai was trapped in Jerusalem, and the Zealots would kill anyone who tried to leave the city, because they were trying to force all Jews to support their rebellion. According to legend, the rabbi devised a ruse. His followers announced that the great rabbi had died from the plague and asked the Zealot leaders for permission to bury him outside the city

Word Work

Diaspora *Diaspora* comes from the Greek word for dispersion. Jews use the term to refer to the period when they were exiled from Israel. It is also used to describe Jewish life and community outside of Israel.

walls to prevent the spread of the dreaded disease. The Zealots agreed, and the rabbi was carried in a coffin out of the city and delivered to the camp of the Roman general Vespasian.

The rabbi emerged from the coffin and told the mighty Roman leader that he had had a prophecy and that he had a request. The rabbi told Vespasian that he would soon be emperor and asked permission to establish a Jewish school. Vespasian agreed to the request on the condition that the prophecy was correct.

The rabbi was right. Vespasian soon became emperor, and he fulfilled his promise and allowed Yochanan ben Zakkai to open his academy in the town of Yavneh, north of Jerusalem, which became the center of Jewish learning for centuries. This innovation helped Judaism survive by ending its dependence on a central Temple and its sacrificial rites. Local synagogues eventually replaced the Temple; prayer replaced sacrificial rites; and an emphasis on Jewish law and education united a scattered community.

Even though the Jewish people were scattered around the globe—in what is referred to as the Diaspora—they never gave up their commitment to their homeland. For more than two thousand years, Jews all over the world dreamed of returning to re-establish an independent Jewish state in the Land of Israel. This dream was recited three times a day in prayer and on every holiday.

Look Closer

After the Jewish revolt in 132 CE, the Romans renamed Judea Palaestina because, according to some scholars, they wanted to minimize Jewish identification with the Land of Israel. The first use of the term *Palestine* goes back to the ancient Greek historian Herodotus in the fifth century BCE. The Arabic word *Filastin* is derived from the Latin name Palaestina. The name is believed to come from an extinct ancient sea people known as the P'lishtim (Philistines). Recent scholarship traces their arrival in the Levant region to the twelfth century BCE, as recorded in Egyptian accounts.

> *Israel matters to me because it's the only place where I can see, touch, and feel the history of my people.*
>
> JESSICA, AGE 32, HIGHLAND PARK, NEW JERSEY

CHAPTER THREE

THE BIRTH OF TWO RELIGIONS

The history of Israel and the Jewish people cannot be told without examining the birth of Christianity and Islam, two of the world's major religions that arose in the same area of the world and that share major characteristics with Judaism. All three religions worship one God, and all three honor Abraham and other Jewish patriarchs and prophets.

THE RISE OF CHRISTIANITY

The Christian faith is deeply rooted in the teachings and identity of a Jewish rabbi, Jesus of Nazareth, who was born in Judea during Roman rule, about 4 BCE, according to scholarly research. The public ministry of Jesus began when he was around thirty years old and was baptized by a man called John the Baptist. For about three years, Jesus moved through the region of Galilee and into Jerusalem, preaching, offering healing, and gaining disciples. Twelve of Jesus's disciples, who were chosen to carry on his mission, were known as the apostles. The gospel of Jesus emphasized the Jewish tradition of justice and compassion as taught by the prophets.

> ## Word Work
>
> **prophet** *Prophets* are believed to be individuals chosen by God to disclose God's will and to lead the people to repentance and observance of God's laws.
>
> **Sanhedrin** A *Sanhedrin* was a Jewish court; courts were located in every city in ancient Judea. The Great Sanhedrin was a kind of Supreme Court that had 71 members and met in the Temple in Jerusalem. This was the highest religious and legal authority in Jewish life.

Jesus grew very popular, and many of his followers began to speak of him as the king of the Jews and the Messiah. According to Christian tradition, Jesus had a conflict with people who were using the Temple for commercial purposes, and Jewish high priests from the Sanhedrin turned Jesus over to the Roman governor, Pontius Pilate, who ordered him crucified. Jesus's followers declared that he rose from the dead on the third day after his Crucifixion, and they began to teach that Jesus was the son of God.

The followers of Jesus eventually became known as Christians, and though their religious practices initially were very similar to Jewish practices, Christian teachers, such as Paul, gradually set forth a doctrine that moved away from some of the most basic tenets of Judaism, such as circumcision. Christians through the centuries have taught that Jesus was the Messiah promised by God in the

Word Work

Messiah *Messiah* is derived from the Hebrew word *Mashiach*, meaning "one who is anointed." "Jesus Christ" is Greek for "Joshua the Messiah." Jews and Christians have different conceptions of the Messiah. The Jewish view of the Messiah is that of an earthly redeemer, instructed by God to bring justice and peace to the world. The Christian understanding of the Messiah is that of the divine redeemer, manifesting God's presence on earth.

Hebrew Bible; Jews believe Jesus was a great teacher but not the Messiah. The Christian faith spread across the Roman Empire, although the Romans frequently persecuted Christians and put them to death by the thousands, in part because they refused to worship the Roman emperor.

However, in 313 CE, the Roman emperor Constantine converted to Christianity and declared it to be a legal religion in the Roman Empire. In 330, Constantine moved the capital of the empire from Rome to the city of Byzantium (what is now Istanbul, Turkey), which he renamed Constantinople. By the late fourth century CE, the Land of Israel had become a predominantly Christian country. Churches were built on Christian holy sites in Jerusalem, Bethlehem, and Galilee, and monasteries were established in many parts of the country. Eventually, Christianity became the official religion of the Roman Empire, making much of what is today Europe and parts of Asia predominantly Christian nations. Jews in those areas were often isolated and persecuted for not accepting the Christian faith.

Even after Rome and the western half of the Roman Empire fell, the Christian church survived, and, in fact, much of the government of Europe for centuries revolved around the Christian church.

The Christian church also lived on, in a slightly different form, in the eastern portions of the empire, where Byzantine emperors succeeded in keeping their empire intact for one thousand years. During that time, however, its size grew and shrank in part because of a new faith that would soon grow in power and influence.

Word Work

Allah *Allah* is the Arabic term for God. Arabs frequently use the word *inshallah*, meaning "if God wills," which suggests that whatever happens in life will be a result of God's will.

ISLAM IS BORN

The founder of Islam, Muhammad, was born in Mecca on the Arabian Peninsula in approximately 570 CE. He was a member of the Quraysh tribe. As with Moses and Jesus, we know little about his childhood. We do know that when he was twenty-five, Muhammad married a widow named Khadija, who was a successful merchant.

Muhammad occasionally withdrew to a cave outside Mecca to meditate and pray for guidance. According to the Islamic faith, when Muhammad was about forty years old, during one of these visits, he had a miraculous encounter with the angel Gabriel, who revealed to him a message in Arabic from God, known as Allah. Muhammad continued to have revelations and believed that he had been chosen as a prophet and therefore began to develop a code of behavior that he said

Look Closer

Semite is a term that was first used in the late eighteenth century for those who descended from Noah's son Shem, but today it commonly identifies people who speak a Semitic language.

However, the terms *anti-Semite* or *anti-Semitic* almost always are used to describe words or actions that oppose Jewish people.

Arabs live throughout the Middle East and North Africa but are called Arabs because of their long-standing presence in Arabia—what is now Saudi Arabia. The majority of Arabs are Muslims, but some are Christians or of other faiths. The majority of Muslims, which include people in Iran and Indonesia, are not Arabs.

had been given him by Allah. The people who accepted Muhammad's teachings came to be known as Muslims, and their religion is called Islam, Arabic for "surrender to the will of Allah." Muhammad is regarded by Muslims as the last and most perfect prophet.

The Holy Koran

Upon Muhammad's death, his followers recorded the prophet's divine revelations, and the written record became known as the Koran. Because God is believed to be the author, the Koran is considered infallible. During the centuries after Muhammad's death, the laws of Islam were codified in the Sharia, Arabic for "the way," and the Hadith, the traditions relating to the words and deeds of Muhammad. The Sharia sets forth laws that regulate Muslim life, some of which appear explicitly in the Koran. These rules are believed to be an expression of God's will but are also subject to the interpretation of Islamic scholars.

Like early Christians, Muhammad and his followers were persecuted for their beliefs. After learning of a plot to murder him, Muhammad and his followers left Mecca in 622 for an oasis then known as Yathrib. To commemorate Muhammad's association with the city, its name was later changed to Medina, which means "City of the Messenger of God." This trip became known as the Hegira, the flight from persecution in Mecca.

Medina also had a sizable Jewish population, most likely descendants of people who had moved there after being expelled from Judea, later Palestine, by the Romans after the destruction of the Second Temple in 70 CE. Muhammad respected the Jews, and his early teachings are similar to those of the Jewish tradition, but when the Jews did not accept him as a prophet, Muhammad began to minimize the

Look Closer

Muhammad's birthplace, Mecca, is considered the most sacred of the Muslim holy cities. Muslims face Mecca during their daily prayers and are obligated to make a pilgrimage there once in their lifetimes. Medina is considered the second most holy city in Islam.

Faces of Israel

Taoufik, sixteen, is an Arab Israeli who was
born and raised in the Arab city of Taibe,
located in northeastern Israel. He has three brothers and one sister. Taoufik
loves to play soccer with his friends at school and was very proud when
his favorite team, B'nei Sakhnin, which has Jewish and Arab players, won
Israel's championship for the first time in 2004.

Taoufik also loves computers and spends a lot of time chatting online with
other Israelis and with Arabs from neighboring countries. Taoufik hopes to
study computer engineering and to travel abroad in the future.

Jewish influence on his beliefs. For example, he shifted the direction of
prayers from Jerusalem to Mecca, made Friday his special day of prayer, and
renounced the Jewish dietary laws (except for the prohibition on eating
pork). As Muhammad's influence began to grow, he came into conflict with
Jewish tribes in Medina and ultimately expelled two of them. His troops
murdered all the male members of a third Jewish tribe and sold the women
and children into slavery.

Creating an Empire

After the death of Muhammad in 632 CE, his followers marched out of
Arabia and proceeded to create a great empire stretching across the Middle
East (including the Land of Israel) and North Africa into Spain. In 638 CE,
the Jews of Palestine assisted Muslim forces in defeating the Persians, who
had reneged on an agreement to protect the Jews and allow them to resettle
in Jerusalem. As a reward for their assistance, the Muslims permitted the Jews
to return to Jerusalem.

Word Work

dhimma *Dhimma* was a classification granting special status to Christians and Jews in Muslim countries. Muslims had particular respect for Jews and Christians, accepting Moses and Jesus as prophets. The concept of the *dhimma* (writ of protection) gave the dhimmis certain rights denied other minorities but still made clear they were viewed as inferior to Muslims.

People of the Book

When Muslims conquered an area, the people in the land often chose to convert to Islam because they accepted the teachings of the Koran or because they did not want to face the restrictions placed on non-Muslims. Sometimes conquered populations were given the choice of death or conversion. But Jews and Christians were treated differently because Muslims saw them as "People of the Book," who adhered to the teachings of the scriptures. So they were allowed to practice their faith but were part of a special category called "dhimmis."

Muslim conquerors were expected to protect dhimmis, but they didn't always treat them well. In fact, dhimmis were considered infidels—people who did not accept Islam—

STRAIGHT from the Source

"The ruler of Baghdad, whose name was al-Muqtadi, directed that yellow badges should be affixed to the headgear of every Jewish male. In addition to the badge on the head, another of lead, the weight of a silver coin, was to hang around the neck of every Jew. He also imposed that every Jew should wear a distinguishing belt around his waist. Each woman had to wear one red shoe and one black shoe. Furthermore, each woman had to have a small copper bell on her neck or on her shoe which would tinkle so that all would know and differentiate between the women of the Jews and of the Muslims."

— WRITER DESCRIBING THE TREATMENT OF JEWS IN THE ELEVENTH CENTURY, QUOTED IN
THE JEWS OF ARAB LANDS, BY NORMAN STILLMAN

Look Closer

The Koran contains expressions promoting tolerance, and specifically praises Jews and Christians who lead virtuous lives, stating that they will be rewarded by their Lord.

and the Muslim rulers expected them to acknowledge the superiority of the true believer—the Muslim. Jews were treated differently from country to country, but, typically, Jews were excluded from public office and armed service, and they were forbidden to bear arms. They were not allowed to pray in loud voices because that might offend the Muslims. They were not permitted to ride horses or camels, to build synagogues taller than mosques, to construct houses higher than those of Muslims, or to drink wine in public.

Jewish communities in Arab and Islamic countries fared better overall than those in Christian lands in Europe, and at various times Jews in Muslim lands were able to live in relative peace and thrive culturally and economically. But Jews were no strangers to persecution and humiliation by the Arabs and Muslims, and their position was never secure. Changes in the political or social climate would often lead to persecution, violence, and death.

Look Closer

The Jewish community made many great developments in philosophy, science, mathematics, medicine, and other disciplines in Spain during the period of Muslim rule from 950 to 1150 CE. The period is often referred to as the Golden Age of Spanish Jewry.

The Crusades

Jews and Muslims found themselves fighting a common enemy in 1095 CE, when Pope Urban II called on Christians to regain Palestine from "the infidels." Thousands of Christians, who became known as Crusaders, responded, attacking Muslims and Jews in the area and capturing Jerusalem in 1099. They murdered almost every inhabitant of Jerusalem—Muslims, Jews, and even some Christians. Non-Christians were subsequently barred from the city.

In 1174, the ruler of Egypt, Saladin, launched his own campaign to take control over much of

Look Closer

The Crusades were a series of military campaigns launched against the Muslims by Western European Christians in an effort to recapture what they considered the Holy Land, the area where Jesus had lived and been crucified and where the Christian church had begun. The First Crusade took place from 1095 to 1099 CE. The ninth and last crusade in the Middle East took place from 1271 to 1272 CE.

the region. He called on fellow Muslims to join him in a war to drive the Christians out of the Holy Land. His army, called Saracens by the Christians, recaptured Jerusalem in 1187. The Christians tried one more time to retake Jerusalem but failed, and Christian rule came to an end in the Middle East.

Although Palestine was ravaged by fighting in a series of Crusades for two centuries, the Jews remained entrenched, living in at least fifty cities in the eleventh century, including Ramleh, Tiberias, Gaza, Ashkelon, Caesarea, and Jerusalem. After the Christians were ultimately defeated, Muslim rulers returned, and the next seven centuries were relatively quiet ones for the Jews in the region. The Jewish population was small and generally tolerated as dhimmis by the succession of Muslim rulers who controlled Palestine.

CHAPTER FOUR

THE RISE OF ZIONISM

The history of the Jewish Diaspora between the years of the Crusades and the nineteenth century is complex. Many Jewish thinkers traveled to the Land of Israel and stayed, including Mosheh ben Nachman, also referred to as Nachmanides or the Ramban, a Spanish rabbi and Bible commentator.

In many communities around the world, Jewish intellectual creativity thrived, and the culture of the host country influenced Jewish thought. For

Word Work

pogrom A *pogrom* is an organized attack on a minority group in which people are murdered and their property destroyed. The term is usually applied to massacres against Jews, particularly a series of murderous attacks that took place in Russia in the 1880s and the decades that followed.

example, many customs associated with the Jewish holiday of Purim originated in Christian Germany. Yet during this time, many Jews were persecuted, unfairly taxed, and banned from various occupations. In Italy, during the Reformation, Jews were unable to work as lawyers, pharmacists, painters, politicians, or architects. They were expelled from Spain in 1492 and from individual cities, such as Prague, during parts of the eighteenth century.

In spite of all these hardships, Jews flourished in many places throughout the ages. They became leaders in fields such as banking, medicine, and philosophy. And yet many Jews found that they couldn't always fit in, no matter how hard they tried. Those who found it difficult to remain Jewish hid their Jewish identity; some stopped practicing Jewish traditions altogether.

Throughout history, however, Jews learned they couldn't escape their identity. When they became too successful, they were often persecuted and forced to leave their homes. When Christians and people of other faiths needed someone

STRAIGHT from the Source

"We further order in this edict that all Jews and Jewesses of whatever age that reside in our domain and territories leave with their sons and daughters, servants and relatives large or small, of all ages, by the end of July of this year, and that they dare not return to our lands and that they do not take a step across, such that if any Jew who does not accept this edict is found in our kingdom and domains or returns will be sentenced to death and confiscation of all their belongings."

—Excerpt from Alhambra Decree ordering the expulsion of Jews from Spain in 1492

to blame for their troubles, they would often fault the Jews. Sometimes religious leaders taught their followers to hate those who were different, and the Jews were always different. As a result, Jews in Europe, even those who assimilated, were often subject to persecution, pogroms, and, ultimately, the Holocaust.

Through these troubled centuries, Jews never gave up the hope of returning to their homeland. In fact, their desire for their own country was strengthened as Jews learned to live without freedom in lands that weren't their own and where they were often denied the rights of citizenship.

THE ZIONIST IDEA

In the nineteenth century, Jewish philosophers began to argue the case for Jews to have a homeland of their own, where they could control their own fate—and they believed the place for that haven was their ancestral home in the Land of Israel.

As some Jews began to leave Europe for Palestine, Zionism emerged as a political movement, spearheaded by Theodor Herzl, a Viennese journalist who had witnessed the evils of anti-Semitism in France when a Jew named Alfred Dreyfus was sent to prison for a crime he didn't commit. This experience convinced Herzl that if Jews were not safe in a country as enlightened as France, they could not be safe anywhere except in a homeland of their own.

Herzl believed the Jewish people were a nation like any other, with a distinct civilization and language, and should have self-determination in their homeland. His book, *The Jewish State*, outlined how such a state should be formed, and Herzl founded the

STRAIGHT from the Source

In 1878, Naphtali Herz Imber wrote the words to "Hatikvah" ("The Hope"), a song expressing the Jewish people's longing for freedom in their homeland. It later became Israel's national anthem:

In the Jewish heart
A Jewish spirit still sings
And the eyes look east toward Zion.
Our hope is not lost
Our hope of two thousand years,
To be a free nation in our land,
In the land of Zion and Jerusalem.

Have You Heard of Theodor Herzl? (1860-1904)

Herzl was born in Budapest, Hungary. A non-religious Jew, Herzl grew sensitive to anti-Semitism while working in Paris as a correspondent for a Vienna newspaper covering the Dreyfus affair. With his charisma, political skill, and access to influential people, Herzl was able to unite and invigorate a fractured and weak Zionist movement.

In 1897, Herzl chaired the first of six Zionist Congresses and founded the World Zionist Organization, serving as its president until his death. In his early years, Herzl was prepared to accept a British plan to establish Uganda as a temporary homeland for the Jewish people. Later he came to believe the Land of Israel was the only place where a Jewish state could be established.

Herzl died almost half a century before his dream became a reality, but his remains were brought to Israel on September 18, 1949, and buried on Mount Herzl in Jerusalem.

World Zionist Organization (WZO) to promote the movement. In 1897, the WZO held its first conference in Basel, Switzerland, and announced that the goal of the Zionist movement was the creation of a Jewish state in Palestine.

Types of Zionism

While Herzl led a political movement to win international recognition for the creation of a Jewish state, other Zionists focused on different aspects of rebuilding the Jewish nation. For example, Practical Zionists focused their efforts on settling the land. Religious Zionists believed the Jewish homeland should be

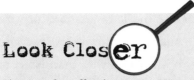

The Dreyfus affair began in 1894 when Alfred Dreyfus, a Jewish officer in the French army, was accused of passing secret French military documents to the German embassy in Paris. Dreyfus was convicted of treason and condemned to life in prison. In 1896, the head of French military intelligence discovered that another French officer was the real traitor, but the evidence was concealed.

Supporters of Dreyfus demanded a new investigation, but opponents insisted Dreyfus and his backers were traitors. Attacks on Dreyfus and the Jewish community were often rooted in anti-Semitic ideas. When Theodor Herzl saw these attacks and this unjust treatment in "enlightened" France, he concluded that anti-Semitism was incurable and that the only place where Jews could be safe was in a state of their own.

Eventually, Dreyfus received a new trial but was found guilty a second time. However, soon after, Dreyfus was pardoned and released, and he was formally exonerated in 1906, when the French Supreme Court annulled his second conviction.

based on Jewish law. Socialist Zionists were particularly interested in matters of communal living, social justice, and equality. Labor Zionists emphasized the importance of working the land and living a life close to nature. Cultural Zionists placed a higher value on Jewish identity and history. Messianic Zionists thought that establishing a Jewish state would help to usher in the messianic age. Some Christians also became adherents of Zionism, sharing the Jewish belief in the right of the Jews to live and rule in their homeland.

However, a small number of Jews adopted an anti-Zionist position because they feared they would be accused of disloyalty to the countries in which they lived. Others opposed Zionism on religious grounds, believing the Messiah had

Word Work

Zionism *Zionism* was a term coined by an Austrian journalist, Nathan Birnbaum, in 1890. It comes from Zion, the original name of the Jebusite stronghold in Jerusalem. Zion became a symbol for Jerusalem during the reign of King David. The goal of Zionism is the political and spiritual renewal of the Jewish people in its ancestral homeland, and a Zionist is someone who supports this objective. To some, a true Zionist Jew is a person who makes *aliyah* and moves to Israel.

to arrive before the Jews could return to their homeland. And many European Jews chose to immigrate to America rather than Israel to pursue other opportunities. In the United States, Louis Brandeis made the case that it was not necessary to live in Israel to be a Zionist. He championed the idea that Zionist and American ideals were similar and that it was possible to be a good Jew, a good American, and a Zionist.

Jewish Connection to the Land

Jews have three important connections to the Land of Israel: biblical, historical, and spiritual. The spiritual link helped sustain Jews during the long centuries of exile and nurtured them in times of persecution.

Today, Jews living in the United States or other countries may not even realize the religious ties that bind them to the Land of Israel. For example, the celebration of many Jewish festivals is based in Israel's geography and culture: The biblical festivals of Sukkot, Pesach, and Shavuot correspond to the harvest times in Israel. The story of the Maccabees' revolt against the Greeks in ancient Israel is retold each year at Hanukkah. Tu BiShevat is marked at the time when plants bloom in Israel, and prayers for rain are recited in the Diaspora during Israel's rainy season.

> **Because of Israel I have a place to go to if my country ever abandons me. This is the land of my ancestors. This is the land of my people.**
>
> NATALIE, AGE 16,
> BLOOMFIELD, MICHIGAN

The Importance of Jerusalem

Jerusalem, the ancient capital of Israel, is the place where the two Jewish Temples once stood. According to the Book of Kings, the First Temple (also known as Solomon's Temple) housed the Ark of the Covenant, which contained the tablets of the Ten Commandments. The First Temple became the focus of Jewish ritual for roughly four hundred years. According to one ancient source, the Ark disappeared when

STRAIGHT from the Source

When approached by a student at Harvard in 1968 who verbally attacked Zionism, Martin Luther King Jr. responded: "When people criticize Zionists, they mean Jews. You're talking anti-Semitism."

Have You Heard of Rabbi Abraham Isaac Kook? (1865–1935)

Kook was born in Latvia and moved to Palestine in 1904, where he became rabbi of Jaffa. Kook's early fervent support of the Zionist movement was a break from traditional Orthodox Jewish thinking and helped establish modern religious Zionism. He was appointed chief rabbi of Jerusalem after World War I and the first chief rabbi of Palestine in 1921.

Kook was a great rabbinic scholar, kabbalist, and political leader who believed that the messianic era was at hand. In 1924, Kook established a yeshiva in Jerusalem that uniquely combined the study of religious teachings and Zionism.

the Babylonians razed Jerusalem, destroyed the First Temple, and exiled most of the Jews in 586 BCE.

When the Persians swept through the region and conquered the area about seventy years later, the Jews were allowed to return to the Land of Israel. With renewed faith, the Jews reconstructed the Temple on the same site of Solomon's magnificent building. This Second Temple was later greatly expanded by the Jewish king Herod and remained the focal point of religious life until it was destroyed by the Romans in 70 CE.

Since that time, even as most Jews were exiled from the area, Jerusalem has remained the focus of the Jewish people's spiritual bond to Israel. Three times a day for two thousand years Jews have prayed for a return to Jerusalem and have repeated the psalmist's oath: "If I forget you, O Jerusalem, let my right hand forget its cunning" (Psalms 137:5).

When Jews pray, they face in the direction of Jerusalem. When Jews wed, the groom breaks a glass in memory of the destruction of the Temple. Many Jews fast on the tenth day of the Hebrew month of Tevet to mark the beginning of the Babylonian siege of Jerusalem and on the seventeenth day of the Hebrew

Look Closer

On the same spot in Jerusalem where, according to the Hebrew Bible, Abraham was supposed to sacrifice his son Isaac, and on which the Temple later stood, Muslims believe Muhammad was carried to the throne of God by the angel Gabriel. In 691 CE, the Dome of the Rock was built on this site, today known as the Temple Mount. Often mistakenly referred to as a mosque, the Dome is a shrine.

Muhammad instructed his followers to visit the "farthest mosque," which is also on the Temple Mount. This mosque, known as Al-Aqsa, is the third holiest place in Islam after Mecca and Medina.

month of Tammuz to remember when the Romans breached the city's walls. In observance of Tisha B'Av, Jews mourn the destruction of the Temple. One of the modern additions to the Jewish calendar is Yom Yerushalayim (Jerusalem Day), the twenty-eighth day of the Hebrew month of Iyar, which marks the date on which the city was reunited by Israeli forces during the 1967 Six-Day War.

OTTOMAN RULE

When the Zionists began advocating for land in the nineteenth century, the area they considered home, the ancient Land of Israel, was officially a part of the Ottoman Empire—as it had been since the beginning of the sixteenth century, when Turkish Muslim warriors swept through the Middle East and absorbed what is now Egypt, Syria, and Western Arabia into their empire.

In the beginning, the Ottoman Empire had a tolerant attitude toward the Jews, and numerous Jewish communities flourished in Palestine, particularly in Jerusalem, Tiberias, Hebron, and Safed. But soon, the Turks valued Palestine only as a source of revenue; so, like many of their predecessors, they neglected the area but began to impose oppressive taxes on the Jews living in the region. Neglect and oppression gradually took their toll, and the Jewish population declined to roughly seven thousand by the end of the sixteen hundreds.

Word Work

Orthodox Judaism

Orthodox Judaism is the form of Judaism characterized by allegiance to strict observance of the laws in the Torah as interpreted in the Talmud and other rabbinic writings. Orthodox Jews regard the Torah as divinely revealed.

The Jewish population did not begin to recover until Orthodox Jews and the first Zionists from Eastern Europe started to move to Palestine in the late eighteen hundreds. Many of these thousands of Jewish immigrants were fleeing anti-Semitism in Europe and Russia. The first modern Jewish settlement in Palestine, Petach Tikva, was founded in 1878.

This first wave of about twenty thousand Jews who arrived in Palestine in the 1880s is referred to as the First Aliyah. *Aliyah,* which

Have You Heard of Aharon David Gordon? (1856-1922)

Usually referred to by his initials, A. D. Gordon was born in Russia. Though he had never been a manual laborer, he decided at age forty-seven to move to Palestine to become a farmer. He ultimately made his home in Degania, the first kibbutz in Israel.

Gordon became known for his philosophy that physical labor and agriculture were the source of a spiritual life and that working the land was a sacred task, not only for an individual but for the entire Jewish people. Agriculture, he believed, would unite the Jewish people with the land and justify the continued existence of the Jewish people there.

"The Land of Israel," he said, "is acquired through labor, not through fire and not through blood." Gordon became the inspiration for a generation of Labor Zionists.

means "ascension" or "going up," refers to the arrival of Jews, as individuals or groups, to live in the Land of Israel.

Early Pioneers

A new series of pogroms in Russia at the beginning of the twentieth century brought a second wave (Second Aliyah) of forty thousand Jewish immigrants to Israel between 1904 and 1914. These pioneers started newspapers, created the first self-defense organization to protect themselves from Arab attack, and revived the Hebrew language, which had, for many generations before, been restricted to use in prayers but now was adopted as the everyday method of communication. Among these early arrivals were many of the Socialist Zionists, who founded the first agricultural collectives known as *kibbutzim*.

The Kibbutz

A kibbutz (plural, *kibbutzim*) is a unique environment in which people live and work together in a shared, cooperative community. In the traditional kibbutz, members jointly own property and have equal responsibilities for maintaining the collective. The kibbutzniks, as people who lived on *kibbutzim* were called, were passionate about the value of manual labor and believed they were building a new nation of Israel with their own hands.

The original *kibbutzim* were agricultural, and members took turns performing the tasks required to run the farm—from feeding animals and picking crops to doing laundry and cooking meals. Children didn't stay with their parents but

Faces of Israel

Ariel, seventeen, is the fifth generation of his family to live on his kibbutz near Tiberias. His great-great-grandparents were pioneers who came from Eastern Europe to cultivate the land of Israel. Ariel's grandfather was killed during the War of Independence, and Ariel was named after him.

Ariel, who has an older sister and a younger brother, enjoys working with many of the animals on the kibbutz and reading books. In the winter, he loves to travel to the nearby Golan Heights to ski. At school, Ariel's favorite subjects are biology and chemistry, and he hopes to go to medical school after he completes his military service.

Although he loves the communal life of the kibbutz, Ariel dreams of living in Tel Aviv, where he can go to the beach during the day and clubs at night.

Word Work

moshav The *moshav* is another unique institution in Israel. On this type of cooperative, the farms are owned by individuals who keep the profits from their labors, but members share the cost of purchasing supplies and marketing what they produce.

lived in their own buildings, where they were educated together and took turns at various jobs suited to their ages. Children grew up knowing the value and importance of work and were taught that all must do their share.

Today, most *kibbutzim* have expanded their activities beyond agriculture to other industries, such as tourism. *Kibbutzim* have long been known for hosting volunteers from around the world who want to experience the unique lifestyle, so a number of *kibbutzim* have created guest houses for tourists and now offer recreational facilities such as swimming pools, horseback trails, and tennis courts. Ideas about the collective culture have also changed on most *kibbutzim*. Children now live with their parents, and elements of capitalism have been integrated, as members have been given more opportunities to acquire personal property and individual wealth.

> "Israel is a beacon of hope, a shining example of what can be accomplished through teamwork, dedication, and chutzpah...Israel shows people around the world the beauty that even a desert can become."
>
> CORY, AGE 20,
> JACKSON, NEW JERSEY

CHAPTER FIVE

CARVING OUT A HOMELAND

As early Jewish pioneers moved to Palestine at the beginning of the twentieth century and focused on growing crops and establishing communities, Zionist politicians continued to fight for the formal establishment of a Jewish state in the region ruled by the disintegrating Ottoman Empire. Even as the Zionists pushed for a homeland, several European countries were vying for control of the area, especially Great Britain. As World War I began, the British and French were determined to dismantle the

Ottoman Empire and expand their own growing empire in the Middle East. To achieve their goals, they began negotiating with both Zionists and Arabs in regard to Palestine and the surrounding areas, exploring ways to seize power.

Chaim Weizmann, a Russian-born Englishman, became the leader of the Zionist movement after Herzl died in 1904, and he encouraged the British to support the creation of a Jewish state in Palestine. The British were interested in helping the Zionists, but mostly for their own reasons. They especially hoped that if American Jews saw Britain helping to create a Jewish homeland, then those Jews might prod US leaders to join the fight against the Germans in World War I. The Zionists believed they had won a great victory when, on November 2, 1917, the British issued a letter from Lord Arthur Balfour, foreign secretary to Lord Walter Rothschild, which came to be known as the Balfour Declaration:

Have You Heard of Chaim Weizmann? (1874-1952)

Born in Motol, Russia, in 1874, Weizmann received his education in biochemistry in Switzerland and Germany. In 1905 he moved to England and was elected to the General Zionist Council. Weizmann's scientific assistance to the Allied forces in World War I brought him into close contact with British leaders and enabled him to play a key role in encouraging the Balfour Declaration. In 1921 Weizmann was elected president of the World Zionist Organization.

Almost thirty years later, in 1947, Weizmann addressed the United Nations General Assembly and influenced US president Harry Truman to recognize Israel. Weizmann became the first president of Israel in 1949, serving until his death in 1952. Today, one of Israel's premier scientific research institutions, the Weizmann Institute, is named after him.

His Majesty's Government view with favour the establishment
in Palestine of a national home for the Jewish people, and will
use their best endeavours to facilitate the achievement of this
object, it being clearly understood that nothing shall be done
which may prejudice the civil and religious rights of existing
non-Jewish communities in Palestine, or the rights and political status enjoyed by Jews in any other country.

But the British also believed they needed help from the Arabs in Arabia to
defeat the Ottomans and made promises to their key leaders even while they
were making promises to the Zionists. The
British high commissioner for Egypt, Sir Henry
McMahon, secretly negotiated with one of the
key leaders of the Arabs, Hussein ibn Ali. If ibn
Ali would lead his people in a revolt against the
Ottoman Empire, McMahon promised, the
Arabs would be granted independence in territories taken away from the Turks. Ibn Ali
agreed, and he and some of his followers were
involved in a revolt against the Turks that
helped lead to their downfall.

Look Closer

The Arab connection to
Palestine did not begin until
after the death of Muhammad
in the seventh century, and
most Palestinian Arabs arrived
in the late nineteenth and
early twentieth centuries.

STRAIGHT from the Source

"I am convinced that this declaration will assure you beyond all possible doubt of
the sympathy of Great Britain toward the aspirations of her friends the Arabs and
will result in a firm and lasting alliance, the immediate results of which will be the
expulsion of the Turks from the Arab countries and the freeing of the Arab peoples
from the Turkish yoke, which for so many years has pressed heavily upon them."

—Excerpt from a letter from Sir Henry McMahon to Hussein ibn Ali

DIVIDING OTTOMAN TERRITORIES

By the time World War I ended in 1917, both Jews and Arabs believed they had been promised self-government in Palestine by the British. The Jews pointed to the Balfour Declaration, while the Arabs said letters exchanged between McMahon and ibn Ali proved their claims to independence. However, Palestine was never mentioned in those letters, and the British subsequently told the Arabs their promises to them had not included Palestine. To complicate matters further, the British and French had made their own secret agreement to divide the Ottoman territories after the war.

THE MANDATES

On April 24, 1920, at a peace conference in San Remo, Italy, France and Great Britain unveiled their agreement, and a system called Mandates was created that allowed France and Great Britain to control the former Ottoman territories. France was given the Mandate for Syria, which included Lebanon, and Great Britain was put in control of Iraq and Palestine. The Mandate for Palestine was formalized by the League of Nations on September 23, 1922.

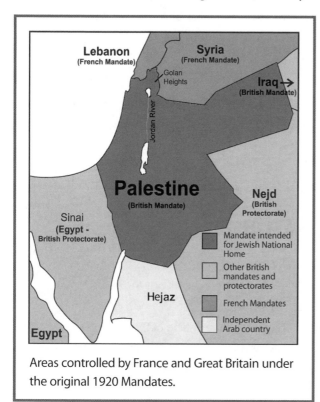

Areas controlled by France and Great Britain under the original 1920 Mandates.

British officials knew many Arabs, especially those who had fought to topple the Turks, had expected an independent state after the war and were infuriated by the Mandates and the Balfour Declaration. Consequently, the British government did everything possible to placate the Arab leaders who had participated in the revolt. To reward one of those Arab leaders, and to prevent the French from expanding their influence in the region, Britain created an entirely new province, severing almost 80 percent of historic Palestine on the eastern bank of the Jordan River and calling it Transjordan. Much of this area is now the country of Jordan.

But the Arabs weren't the only ones who felt betrayed by the British; many Jews felt the British were not living up to their obliga-

Transjordan, the province created by Great Britain in 1923.

Word Work

Mandates *Mandates* were systems created after World War I by the League of Nations, the forerunner to today's United Nations. They allowed member nations to govern former German colonies and other conquered lands, including those in the Middle East that had been part of the Ottoman Empire.

tions of the Balfour Declaration and were especially angry that the British had chopped up the land and given the biggest piece to the Arabs to create Transjordan. Still, the British at first seemed prepared to endorse a national home for the Jewish people, which many Zionists believed would give their community in Palestine greater political legitimacy.

BUILDING A JEWISH STATE

With the official approval of the British, the Jews began developing the structure for a state, including a political body to make deci-

Word Work

Haganah   The *Haganah* was a clandestine Jewish organization for armed self-defense, initiated in Palestine under the British Mandate. This group eventually became the nucleus of the IDF.

Histadrut   The *Histadrut* was the Jewish Labor Federation created in 1920 as a trade union to organize the economic activities of Jewish workers. The Histadrut's goals are to ensure employment and job security for all.

The Jewish Agency   The *Jewish Agency* was established in 1929 as the formal representative of the Jewish community to the British Mandatory government. It gradually became a government in all but name, and its leaders formed the first Israeli government in 1948. After the establishment of the State of Israel, the Jewish Agency became a division of the government that focused on issues common to the state and to Jewish communities abroad.

sions for the community, the expansion of rural and urban development, and, most important, the growth of the population. At the end of World War I, the Jewish population in the land of Palestine was only about ninety thousand, compared with six hundred thousand Arabs. After the war, the Third Aliyah, stimulated largely by the Russian Revolution, brought another forty thousand Jews to the area. This group helped develop the country, draining malarial swamps and building towns. During this period, the underground military defense force known as the Haganah was created, as was the first Jewish labor union, the Histadrut.

In the 1920s, the goal of increasing the Jewish population was again aided by a combination of anti-Semitism and economic hardship, this time primarily in Poland. This fourth wave of immigration brought in about eighty thousand more Jews, mostly from the middle class, who subsequently helped build the economy of Palestine.

Jewish Immigrants to Palestine, 1930-1941

Year	Immigrants
1930	4,944
1931	4,075
1932	12,533
1933	37,337
1934	45,267
1935	66,472
1936	29,595
1937	10,629
1938	14,675
1939	31,195
1940	10,643
1941	4,592

The persecution of Jews in Europe prompted surges of immigration to Palestine.

A final large surge of 250,000 immigrants arrived primarily from Germany and Eastern Europe in the decade from 1929 to 1939. This group, which included many professionals who helped build towns and industry, came largely as a result of Adolf Hitler's persecution of Jews.

ARABS REVOLT

The Arab population of Palestine felt threatened by the increasing Jewish population and perceived these immigrants to be foreigners invading their country and stealing their land. They complained bitterly, first to the Turks, and then to the British Mandatory authorities. The Zionists made some efforts to negotiate with the Arabs and to find a way to coexist but did not succeed in placating the Arabs, who turned to violence, instigated by the religious leader of Jerusalem known as the mufti, Haj Amin al-Husseini.

Beginning in 1921, the mufti of Jerusalem provoked riots against the Jews in an effort to force the British to terminate the Balfour Declaration and restrict Jewish immigration. A major riot in 1929 led to the massacre of Jews from the

Word Work

mufti A *mufti* is a Muslim leader responsible for interpreting Muslim law. A mufti is generally held in high esteem in his community, and his opinion can be expressed in a document called a fatwa.

ancient town of Hebron, where the Jewish patriarchs and matriarchs (Abraham and Sarah, Isaac and Rebecca, and Jacob and Leah) are believed to be buried. The Jews who survived left the city and did not return for more than four decades. In 1936, the Arabs began a more sustained revolt that lasted for three years.

Throughout these years, each time the Arabs rioted, the British would launch an investigation. A commission would go to Palestine and hear Arab complaints that the Jews were stealing their land and driving them out of Palestine. In fact, the Zionists preferred to purchase land that was inexpensive, which usually meant it was uncultivated, swampy, and had no one living on it. By 1930, the Jewish population owned about three hundred thousand acres, of which approximately 40 percent was purchased from foreign landowners and 57 percent from local owners of large estates. Less than one percent was sold by small Arab landowners.

While many local Arabs complained, British commissions found that the Arabs actually benefitted from the rising standing of living and better health care Jewish immigration brought. Some Arabs chose to immigrate to Palestine. The British government's White Papers—statements of British policy—were encouraging to the Arabs because they recommended curtailing Jewish immigration.

Dividing Palestine

After years of trying to forge a peace between Jews and Arabs, a 1937 British commission led by Lord Peel concluded that the best solution to the problem was to divide Palestine into an Arab state and a Jewish state. To British officials, it seemed logical that if two peoples were fighting over one land, it should be divided between them. But the Arabs rejected the plan, declaring they would never share the land with the Jews. Many Jews, under the official leadership of the Yishuv, were willing to accept the compromise solution, but others opposed

Have You Heard of Haj Amin al-Husseini? (1893-1974)

Haj Amin al-Husseini was the most prominent Arab figure in Palestine during the Mandatory period. Al-Husseini was born in Jerusalem in 1893 and went on to serve in the Ottoman Army during World War I. He began to organize groups to terrorize Jews in 1919 in the hope of driving them out of Palestine; in 1920, he was sentenced to ten years in prison by the British for inciting riots against Jews. He fled to Transjordan, but the British pardoned him and allowed him to return to Palestine.

In 1921 he was appointed mufti of Jerusalem by the British, who hoped his appointment would placate the Palestinian Arabs. He used that position to expand his power gradually. One of the mufti's most successful projects was the restoration of the Dome of the Rock and the Al-Aqsa Mosque in Jerusalem.

But al-Husseini provoked violence and bloody riots against Jews in 1929 and 1936 as he campaigned for the unification of Palestine with Syria. The mufti's uncompromising views forced the Zionists to abandon their efforts to reach an agreement with Arabs in Palestine. Following the Arab riots that broke out in 1936, the mufti was dismissed from his position and fled the country. During World War II, the mufti met with Hitler and tried to mobilize Muslim support for the Axis powers but never returned to Palestine or regained his influence.

it because they believed they were entitled to a state in all of Palestine. The British shelved the plan.

One Jewish leader who viewed Peel's partition idea as another step away from the Balfour Declaration was Ze'ev (Vladimir) Jabotinsky, head of the Revisionist

Word Work

Yishuv The Jewish community of Palestine before 1948 was referred to as the *Yishuv*.

Irgun The *Irgun* (Irgun Tzva'i Le'umi, National Military Organization) was founded in Palestine in 1931. This underground Jewish military force fought against both the Arabs and British.

Zionists, who insisted the Jews were entitled to a state in all of the historic land of Israel, including the part that had been sliced away to create Transjordan. Jabotinsky did not believe the British would ever fulfill their promise to create a Jewish homeland and argued that the Jews would have to fight to win their land. Some of his followers split off from the Haganah, which had functioned purely as a self-defense force, and created a more militant organization known as the Irgun, which began to take offensive actions against the Arabs and later the British.

The British Close the Door

With the failure of the Peel Plan, the British returned to their policy of proposing restrictions on Jewish rights to property and immigration. As the Arabs continued to revolt against Zionist advances, Jewish immigration in 1939 more than doubled as Jews fled Nazi Germany and World War II began with the German invasion of Poland.

The British then issued a new White Paper, declaring that the government intended to establish an Arab state in Palestine within ten years. Furthermore, Jewish immigration would be limited to seventy-five thousand people over five years and no immigration would be allowed after that without Arab permission. The policy completely abandoned the Balfour promise and imposed a death sentence for thousands of Jews trying to escape the Nazis.

The British move was in part calculated to prevent the Arabs from supporting Germany at the dawn of World War II. Even though the Jews felt betrayed by the new policy, the British knew they

Think about It

Why did the British restrict the number of Jews entering Palestine, especially after the Holocaust began?

???

Have You Heard of Ze'ev (Vladimir) Jabotinsky? (1880-1940)

Ze'ev (Vladimir) Jabotinsky was born on October 18, 1880, in Odessa, Russia. At the age of eighteen, he left for Italy and Switzerland to study law and later served as a correspondent for several Russian newspapers. The pogrom against the Jews of Kishinev in Russia in 1903 spurred Jabotinsky to undertake Zionist activity.

After the outbreak of World War I, he became a war correspondent, later working for the establishment of a Jewish unit in the British army, the Jewish Legion, and ultimately serving as a lieutenant in it.

In 1920, Jabotinsky was part of the Haganah force defending Jews in Jerusalem against Arab riots. He was arrested by the British for his activities and sentenced to fifteen years of hard labor. Following public outcry against the verdict, he received amnesty and was released. In 1925 he established the Union of Revisionist Zionists, which called for the immediate establishment of a Jewish state in all of historic Palestine, which included Transjordan.

In 1929, he left the country on a lecture tour but was not allowed to return. From outside Palestine, Jabotinsky led three organizations aimed at establishing a state and bringing Jewish immigrants to Israel. The New Zionist Organization maintained contacts with governments and political officials, the youth movement Betar developed support for the establishment of a Jewish state, and the Irgun was the military arm that fought against enemies of the Zionist enterprise.

Before he died in 1940, Jabotinsky requested that his remains be interred in Israel when a Jewish state was created. His wish was granted by Levi Eshkol, Israel's third prime minister, in 1964.

would never support the Nazis, but they were worried that the Arabs would make alliances with Germany, as some ultimately did.

FIGHTING TWO BATTLES

Jews in Palestine were torn. As the war in Europe expanded to a world war, and the fate of the Jews in Europe became more precarious, the Jews in Palestine were determined to fight Hitler. At the same time, they could not tolerate the repudiation of the Balfour Declaration. Therefore, the leader of the Jewish community, David Ben-Gurion, announced, "We must assist the British in the war as if there were no White Paper and we must resist the White Paper as if there were no war."

Many Jews from all over the world joined the fight against the Nazis. Participants from a variety of Zionist organizations also gathered at the Biltmore Hotel in New York in 1942 to reaffirm their commitment to the establishment of a Jewish state and call for unrestricted immigration to Palestine. As the news of the Holocaust began to leak out of Europe, Jews in

Have You Heard of Hannah Senesh? (1921-1944)

A young woman, Hannah Senesh (or Szenes), was a World War II Zionist hero. Responding to anti-Semitism in her native Hungary, Senesh moved to Palestine in 1939. She fought for the Haganah in a special unit that parachuted behind German lines to rescue allied prisoners and organize Jewish partisan activity. Senesh was captured and tortured by the Nazi-controlled Hungarian police. She was tried by a secret court and executed by firing squad on November 7, 1944. Her body was reburied on Mount Herzl in 1950.

Word Work

Mossad The *Mossad*, which is short for *Hamossad L'modi'in U'l'tafkidim Miyuchadim* (the Institute for Intelligence and Special Operations), is the Israeli government's intelligence agency. Originally derived from an organization that brought Jews from Nazi-occupied Europe to Israel, the Mossad's current function is to collect intelligence, conduct covert operations, and fight terrorism.

Palestine did everything they could to smuggle immigrants into the country. The British were equally determined, however, to prevent more Jews than allowed by their quota from entering Palestine.

Even as the Jews were supporting the British fight against the Nazis, some Jews became more militant in their fight against the British in Palestine. A splinter group known as the Stern Gang (after its leader Avraham Stern) or Lehi (a Hebrew acronym) began to terrorize the British and assassinated Lord Moyne, Britain's minister of state for the Middle East, in Cairo in 1944, further enraging the British. The violent attacks by the Irgun and Lehi were condemned by the Jewish leaders in Palestine, who still used the Haganah primarily as a defensive force to protect Jewish communities from attacks by Arabs.

The Battle after the War

When World War II ended, the British made clear they would not implement the Balfour Declaration. They also continued to restrict Jewish immigration to Palestine, preventing now stateless Jewish Holocaust survivors from coming to what they believed was their homeland. Violence escalated as some Jews in the region stepped up attacks on the British, demanding a homeland for the Jewish people.

In the most dramatic attack, the Irgun bombed the British military headquarters in the King David Hotel in Jerusalem in 1946, killing ninety-one people, including Jews and Arabs. Irgun leaders had warned the British of their impending attack, but their early warning was not taken seriously.

Challenges to Immigration

Often ships carrying Jewish immigrants who were trying to get to Palestine were turned back or sunk, or their passengers were arrested and imprisoned on Cyprus. The most famous case, which was immortalized in later years by the Leon Uris novel and subsequent movie, was that of the *Exodus 1947,* a ship that left France on July 11, 1947, carrying forty-five hundred immigrants. It was challenged and boarded by the British Navy, and three Jews were killed. While the world watched in horror, the remaining immigrants were forcibly transported back to Germany in British ships.

But the British could not stop everyone. Thousands of Jews wanted so desperately to return to their homeland that they walked, stowed away, crammed themselves into the holds of unseaworthy ships, and did everything possible to reach their Promised Land. The total number of Jewish immigrants, legal and illegal, from 1922 to 1948 was approximately 480,000. Nearly all came from Europe.

THE UNITED NATIONS

The British people became increasingly distraught by the violence and disturbing scenes coming from Palestine. The Arabs continued attacking the Jews, and now

STRAIGHT from the Source

"Squeezed between a green toilet shed and some steel plates were hundreds and hundreds of half-naked people who looked as though they had been thrown together into a dog pound. Trapped and lost, they were shouting at us in all languages, shattering each other's words. The hot sun filtered through the grillwork, throwing sharp lines of light and darkness across the refugees' faces and their hot, sweaty half-naked bodies. Women were nursing their babies. Old women and men sat weeping unashamed, realizing what lay ahead."

— Journalist Ruth Gruber describing the passengers of the *Exodus* after the ship was ordered to return to Germany

the Jews were fighting back. Previously, the violence in the region had not particularly upset the people in England because their citizens remained largely above the fray; now, however, the Jews were increasingly attacking British targets.

By February 1947, the British government decided to turn the question of what to do with Palestine over to the United Nations, which had been founded in 1945 as an international body to help resolve conflicts between countries. The United Nations sent a delegation to investigate the conflict between Jews and Arabs and listened to their respective positions. At that time, the Arabs constituted a majority of the population in Palestine—1.2 million Arabs versus 600,000 Jews. The Jewish population, however, had been severely limited by the restrictive immigration policy of the British, while the Arabs had been free to come—and thousands did arrive, taking advantage of the rapid development stimulated by Zionist settlement in the first half of the twentieth century.

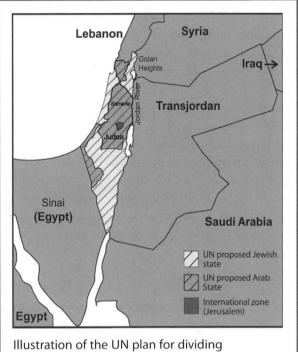

Illustration of the UN plan for dividing Palestine into Arab and Jewish states. The city of Jerusalem was to be declared an international zone.

After studying the situation, the majority of the UN delegates came to the same conclusion as Peel had a decade earlier: The only fair way to resolve the dispute was to divide Palestine into an Arab state and a Jewish state.

Divided Reaction to Idea of Division

Many Western nations were sympathetic to the proposal. Hitler's murderous actions had also persuaded many Western countries that the Jewish people

Look Closer

The UN partition resolution would have failed without the support of the United States. While many members of President Harry Truman's administration opposed the creation of a Jewish state—fearing the move would hurt America's relationship with Arab countries and threaten US oil supplies—nonetheless Truman supported the Zionist movement because he believed the international community was obligated to fulfill the promise of the Balfour Declaration to provide the Jewish survivors of the Holocaust with a home.

needed a home of their own. The United States threw its full weight behind the partition of Palestine and vigorously lobbied nations to support the resolution.

But the Arabs and their allies were bitterly opposed to the plan and demanded a single Arab state in Palestine. Jamal Husseini, a spokesman for the Palestinian Arabs, warned the United Nations that Arabs would fight to prevent the creation of a Jewish state and would drench "the soil of our beloved country with the last drop of our blood."

Although they did not react as violently as the Arabs, many Jews were not enthusiastic about the partition resolution either. They believed the Jewish homeland had already been partitioned when the British had created Transjordan, and they were now being asked to accept statehood in an area that was a fraction of the size of the original land promised by Balfour. Though they were offered about 60 percent of the territory of Palestine excluding Transjordan, most of that was the infertile land of the Negev desert. The population of the Jewish state would consist of 538,000 Jews and 397,000 Arabs, while the Arab state would have 804,000 Arabs and 10,000 Jews.

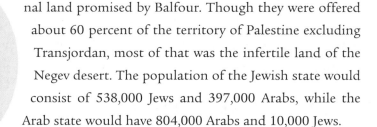

Think about It

Why did the Arabs not want to accept the partition plan?

Furthermore, the UN plan called for the international-ization of Jerusalem to guarantee free access to the holy places of Islam, Christianity, and Judaism. The Jews felt this plan forced them to give up their ancient capital and meant that the 100,000 Jews who lived in the city would be isolated—surrounded by the Arab state that was to encircle the internationalized area.

Think about It

Debate whether or not the Jewish attacks against the British authorities in Palestine were justi-fied; explain your arguments.

? ? ?

Plan Wins Approval

The UN General Assembly approved the partition of Palestine on November 29, 1947, by a vote of 33 to 13, with 10 abstentions.

Despite what the Zionists viewed as an unsatisfactory offer, they decided to accept the plan because it meant the establishment of a Jewish state with the backing of the international community.

The Arabs, however, insisted that they were entitled to all of Palestine and started an undeclared war to prevent the implementation of the UN decision.

CHAPTER SIX

FIGHTING FOR INDEPENDENCE

Though Britain still controlled Palestine, violence broke out almost immediately after the United Nations voted to divide Palestine into Arab and Jewish states. The Arabs openly declared their intention to drive the Jews into the sea and went on the offensive.

In this first phase of this undeclared war, lasting from November 29, 1947, until about April 1, 1948, the Palestinian Arabs inflicted severe casualties on the Jews and disrupted passage along most of their major roadways.

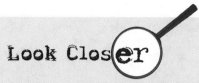

Look Closer

As in any war, many terrible incidents occurred in battles between Jews and Arabs. One of the most notorious involved an effort by fighters from the Irgun and Stern Gang to capture the Arab village of Deir Yassin, which overlooked the highway to Jerusalem and allowed the Palestinians to fire on supply convoys trying to reach the beleaguered city. On April 9, 1948, the two organizations attacked Deir Yassin and killed more than one hundred Arabs, including women and children.

The Arabs accused the Jews of committing a massacre, and the Jewish Agency immediately condemned the attack and apologized. The Arabs publicized what happened at Deir Yassin in the hope of encouraging the Arab states to attack the Jews, but the main impact was to scare many Palestinians and cause them to flee the region.

Four days after the reports from Deir Yassin were published, an Arab force ambushed a Jewish convoy on the way to Hadassah Hospital in Jerusalem, killing seventy-seven Jews, including doctors, nurses, patients, and the director of the hospital. Another twenty-three people were injured.

Arabs blockaded the main road to Jerusalem in an effort to starve the Jews in the Old City. For more than five months, Jews battled Palestinian Arabs and guerrillas infiltrating the country from neighboring states.

Despite initial disadvantages in numbers, organization, and weapons, the Jews began to win the battles. Beginning in April 1948, the Haganah captured several major towns, including Tiberias and Haifa, and temporarily opened the road to Jerusalem.

DECLARING INDEPENDENCE

On May 14, 1948, as the last British troops evacuated, the leadership of the Jewish community formally declared the independence of the State of Israel. That Declaration of Independence spelled out the new state's commitment to the principles of freedom and equality.

The United States was the first to recognize the new state, just eleven minutes after Israel declared its independence. A few hours later, five Arab armies—from Egypt, Syria, Transjordan, Lebanon, and Iraq—invaded Israel.

Have You Heard of Mickey Marcus? (1902-1948)

A colonel in the US Army during World War II, Marcus went to Israel to help the Jewish nation build an army capable of defending the fledgling state. The US War Department gave Marcus permission to go to Israel on condition that he not use his own name or rank. Thus "Michael Stone" was the man who designed a command structure for Israel's new army and wrote training manuals for it.

When the Jewish section of Jerusalem was about to fall, Marcus ordered the construction of the "Burma Road" to break the Arab siege. In gratitude, David Ben-Gurion named Marcus a lieutenant general, the first general in the army of Israel in nearly two thousand years.

Tragically, shortly thereafter, Marcus was accidentally killed by an Israeli soldier. Marcus, who did not speak Hebrew, had failed to respond with the proper password at a checkpoint. Hollywood later immortalized Marcus in the movie *Cast a Giant Shadow*.

Faces of Israel

Aviva, eighteen, was born in the beachfront town of Herzliya. She loves math and sci-ence. In her spare time, Aviva practices violin, which she plays in a string quartet with some other kids at school. She comes from a family of mathe-maticians and wants to work on computers in the army and then study engineering at the Technion, a famous institute of technology in Haifa.

Some of the world's leading high-tech companies, including Motorola and Sony, have offices in her hometown, and Aviva would like to be a software engineer for one of them someday. Eventually, Aviva hopes to start her own business or create her own software, like the three Israelis who devel-oped the system AOL bought to use in its instant messaging service.

Struggling to Survive

Even as Israel formally declared its independence, it knew it had to overcome many obstacles to survive. Israel's leaders thought they were vastly outnum-bered and believed their enemies to be much better armed. (The Arab armies turned out to be smaller than they expected, with more limited weaponry.) On the eve of the war, chief of operations Yigael Yadin told Israel's leader David Ben-Gurion: "The best we can tell you is that we have a 50-50 chance."

When Israel declared its independence, the Israeli army did not have a sin-gle cannon or tank, and nine obsolete planes made up the whole air force. Although the Haganah had sixty thousand trained fighters, fewer than one-third of them were armed and prepared for war, and the Jews were forced to smuggle weapons, principally from Czechoslovakia.

And Israel could not look to the United States for much help. Although the United States vigorously supported the UN partition resolution, the State Department still feared antagonizing the Arabs and did not want to provide the

STRAIGHT from the **Source**

"The State of Israel will promote the development of the country for the benefit of all its inhabitants; will be based on the precepts of liberty, justice, and peace; will uphold the full social and political equality of all its citizens, without distinction of race, creed, or sex; will guarantee full freedom of conscience, worship, education, and culture. We yet call upon the Arab inhabitants of the State of Israel to play their part in the development of the State, with full and equal citizenship."

—FROM ISRAEL'S DECLARATION OF INDEPENDENCE

Jews with weapons to defend themselves. Some diplomats hoped a US refusal to provide arms would prevent the establishment of a Jewish state; President Truman agreed to impose an arms embargo on the region because he hoped it would avert a war.

Some Arab armies had easier access to weapons. In fact, Jordan's Arab Legion was armed and trained by the British and led by a British officer.

The Arab forces aligned against Israel also had vastly larger populations to draw from. They mobilized about eighty thousand men, far fewer than their potential but still more than the Jews could put in the field. And the Arabs also could use the Arab towns and villages in and around the Jewish state as bases of operations. They succeeded in blockading the Old City of Jerusalem for five months, forcing the last Jewish holdouts to surrender on May 29, 1948.

Winning Important Battles

In spite of all these obstacles, Israeli forces eventually turned the tide of the confrontation. Some say that the Arab states never committed their full military might to the war, while the Jews managed to smuggle in enough weapons to defend themselves and became a more effective fighting force as time went on. The Zionists knew that if they lost, their dream of statehood would be over and they could face annihilation. They were able to stop the Arab attacks and defend their

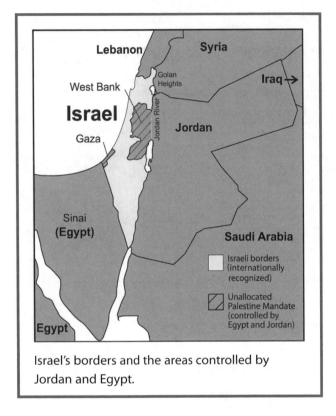

Israel's borders and the areas controlled by Jordan and Egypt.

newborn country, leading most of the Arab countries to sign armistice agreements with Israel in 1949. Because of their successes on the battlefield, the Israelis were able to expand control over territory outside the boundaries originally established by the United Nations, meaning the Arabs now had less territory than they would have had if they had accepted the partition plan without a fight.

The fledgling country was not only winning military battles but political ones as well, since many countries around the world, including the Soviet Union, recognized Israel's right to exist, and the UN Security Council threatened in July 1948 to cite the Arab governments for aggression.

Israel had survived and proved to most of the world that it deserved to exist as an independent state, but the cost of the war was enormous. A total of 6,373 Israelis were killed, nearly 1 percent of the entire Israeli Jewish population at that time.

The War of Independence also created a new dilemma that Israel still struggles with today: Palestinian refugees.

THE REFUGEES

Even before the fighting in Palestine began, a population shift began to occur. Although the doors remained barred by the British until the day of Israel's independence—and to some extent afterward—Jews from around the world tried to

What Would YOU *Do?*

It is April 1948, and you are a Palestinian Arab living in the city of Haifa, the only home you have ever known. The United Nations has said Haifa will be part of a Jewish state. You've always gotten along with your Jewish neighbors, but you are frightened about what could happen if a state is established with Jews in charge.

Arabs from surrounding countries have invaded Palestine to prevent the Jews from declaring independence. The Jews are fighting back, and your leaders say the Jews are trying to kill all Palestinians and steal their land. You have heard that Jews massacred hundreds of peaceful villagers in Deir Yassin. They might do the same if you don't move to a safer place.

Your leaders say you'll be able to return to your homes and also take the property of the Jews when the Jews are defeated. But you have also heard that a Jewish woman named Golda Meir met with some of the elders and tried to persuade them to stay and live in peace in a state governed by Jews.

What Really Happened

In early April 1948, an estimated twenty-five thousand Arabs left the Haifa area following an offensive by Arab forces and rumors that they would soon bomb the Jewish areas. On April 23, the Haganah captured Haifa. A British police report from Haifa, dated April 26, explained that "every effort is being made by the Jews to persuade the Arab populace to stay and carry on with their normal lives, to get their shops and businesses open and to be assured that their lives and interests will be safe."

But many Palestinians were afraid to be judged traitors to the Arab cause or to be caught in the crossfire of the war. By the end of the battle, more than fifty thousand Palestinians had fled Haifa.

make their way to the designated area the United Nations had declared would be a Jewish homeland. By contrast, Palestinian Arabs began to leave that area, first in a trickle and eventually in a flood.

When plans for setting up a state were made in early 1948, Jewish leaders in Palestine had expected the new country of Israel to include a significant Arab population. From the Israeli perspective, the Palestinian Arabs could stay in their homes and be a part of the new state, and approximately 160,000 chose to do so. But many thousands more chose to leave their homes without a clear destination, becoming refugees.

The Palestinians left their homes in 1947 and 1948 for many reasons. Thousands of wealthy Arabs left in anticipation of a war; thousands more responded when Arab leaders warned them to get out of the way of the advancing armies; some were expelled; but most simply fled to avoid being caught in the crossfire of battle. Estimates vary, but approximately 650,000 Palestinians became refugees in this period.

The Mandate Is Carved Up

When the Arab nations went to war to try to block the creation of Israel, Transjordan captured the territory we now know as the Old City of Jerusalem and the West Bank, taking over the main areas the United Nations planned for

STRAIGHT from the Source

"The tragedy of the Palestinians was that most of their leaders had paralyzed them with false and unsubstantiated promises that they were not alone; that 80 million Arabs and 400 million Muslims would instantly and miraculously come to their rescue."

—FROM THE MEMOIRS OF JORDANIAN KING ABDULLAH

an Arab state. The Gaza Strip, another area allotted to the Arab state, was captured by Egypt. By the time the war was over, almost all of Palestine that the United Nations had set aside for Arabs was controlled by Israel or other Arab countries, leaving most of the Palestinian Arabs stateless.

After the war, Israel allowed some Palestinian Arabs who had fled their homes inside the Jewish borders to return. However, for security reasons, most were prevented from re-entering the country. In 1949, Israel offered to allow families that had been separated during the war to return and to repatriate one hundred thousand refugees. The Arabs rejected this and all other Israeli compromises that could be interpreted as recognition of the State of Israel. Instead, they demanded that Israel repatriate all the refugees as a precondition for negotiations, something Israel rejected.

Permanent Refugees

To make matters worse for the Palestinians, the surrounding Arab states refused to resettle the Palestinians in their countries and—with the exception of Jordan—denied them citizenship.

Initially, many of the Palestinian Arabs who fled Israel were confined to refugee camps and became dependent on aid from the international community to survive. The United Nations created an organization to assist them, the UN Relief and Works Agency (UNRWA), which is the only UN organization dedicated solely to the welfare of one group of refugees.

The expectation was that the refugee problem would be settled quickly, as others had been earlier in the century. Israel thought the issue would be resolved as part of a peace agreement, but the Arab states would not negotiate and used the refugees as pawns to remind the world that the Palestinian issue could not be ignored.

To this day, the children, grandchildren, and great-grandchildren of these Palestinian refugees seek to return to their original homes inside what is now Israel, but most of that land is now home to some of the thousands of Jews who immigrated to Israel from all over the world in the years since 1948.

Approximately 820,000 Jews were expelled or forced to flee from Arab countries between 1948 and 1972. Most of these refugees were resettled in Israel and the remainder in other countries. The Arab governments that confiscated their possessions have never offered them any compensation.

Since 1948 the Palestinian refugee crisis has remained a source of conflict in negotiations. Israeli and world leaders have attempted to resolve this issue over the years, but the Arab states and the Palestinians rejected the compromises that were suggested. The quest for Palestinian statehood will be discussed later in the book.

Think about It

How did Israel defeat the Arab countries when the Jews there faced so many obstacles?

???

CHAPTER SEVEN

BUILDING A NEW COUNTRY

hen Israel declared its independence in May 1948, its founders had to decide what type of government it would have. The Jewish population in Palestine had swelled to 650,000 by that time, and most of those Jews had come from Europe. Many of them had formed their political views while living under regimes based on state-run economies.

In the first three decades of state building, the government of Israel owned many of the major industries, such as the airlines, railway, and telephone

Word Work

theocracy   *Theocracy* comes from the Greek *theokratia*, "government by a god." In a theocracy, the country views God as the source of all law and legitimacy and often allows religious authorities to interpret the laws.

Torah   *Torah* in Hebrew literally means "teaching" or "instruction." Torah is sometimes used to describe all Jewish tradition, but the word usually refers specifically to the *Pentateuch*, which is the first five books of the Bible: Genesis, Exodus, Leviticus, Numbers, and Deuteronomy.

halachah   *Halachah* in Hebrew literally means "the path that one walks." *Halachah* refers to the body of Jewish law governing everyday life. Some of these laws appear in the Torah, others in the Talmud and in a sixteenth-century code of behavior known as the *Shulchan Aruch*. Rabbis interpret these laws and apply them to modern life.

companies. As the country matured, however, it adopted an economic model closer to that of the United States, with greater private ownership.

BALANCING RELIGION AND GOVERNMENT

The Zionist leaders, having come from countries where the Jews had been persecuted and often were powerless, wanted their nation to be a democracy. At the same time, they wanted their nation to have strong roots in Judaism. Some Israelis were not religious, while others were very committed to Jewish religious laws, or *halachah*. So the early Israeli leaders needed to find compromises that would allow Jews with different views to live together peacefully as well as ensure that people of other faiths would not face discrimination.

The provisional government of Israel, formed in 1948, included representatives from all the various segments of the Zionist movement. For the sake of

Look Closer

The name Israel is first found in the Bible after Abraham's grandson Jacob struggles all night with an angel. At that point, God declares, "Your name shall be called no more Jacob but Israel, for you have striven with God and with men and prevailed" (Genesis 32:29). Jacob's descendants eventually became known as the children of Israel (Exodus 1:1).

unity, the secular leaders made an agreement with the religious leaders guaranteeing that certain aspects of Jewish law, such as closing state-run businesses on the Jewish Sabbath (Saturday), would be institutionalized in a socialist-Zionist government. As a further concession to the religious community, the leaders agreed that the state would legislate public issues but that private matters—primarily marriage and divorce—would be left to religious courts and that Christians, Muslims, and Jews would each have their own authorities.

Israel has no written constitution because of objections raised by both secular and religious Jews. When a constitution was first proposed in 1949, religious Jews feared it would not be consistent with the laws of Judaism. They argued that a constitution would not be necessary, because *halachah* was essentially the Jewish constitution. But nonreligious Jews didn't believe the country should be governed by the religious laws because that would mean Israel would become a theocracy—a state governed by religious leaders and laws—rather than a democracy. From the day of independence to the present, Israel has struggled with this tension.

Ultimately, the Knesset—the Israeli parliament—passed a series of Basic Laws that guaranteed most of the same rights as those set forth for Americans in the Bill of Rights of the US Constitution. Despite the identification of Israel as a Jewish state, for example, freedom for all religions is guaranteed. Israel also provides for freedom of the press, assembly, and speech.

Think about It

What are the advantages and disadvantages of having two major political parties, as in the United States, compared to the multiparty system, such as we see in Israel?

? ? ?

PROPORTIONAL REPRESENTATION

Israeli leaders established the country as a parliamentary democracy, which operates somewhat differently than the system in the United States. In national elections, which are held at least once every four years, political parties present lists of candidates for the 120-seat Knesset, which is similar to the US Congress. Those seats are divided up among the parties in proportion to the number of votes tallied for each party.

For example, if Party A receives 40 percent of the vote, 48 members of that party are seated in the Knesset. If Party B receives 30 percent, 36 representatives would get Knesset seats, while Party C and Party D each get 18 seats because their parties each received 15 percent of the vote. It isn't difficult to start a political party in Israel, so there are many parties that represent a wide range of perspectives. To win a seat in the Knesset, however, the party has to win a minimum number of votes.

Look Closer

The president of Israel is elected by the Knesset, but the post primarily carries ceremonial powers. The Knesset also has the power to legislate and adopt laws based on the will of the ruling government. The prime minister has more power than an American president because the majority of Knesset members are from the party of the prime minister and other parties in the government; consequently, most foreign and domestic policy is determined by the executive branch. Like members of the Knesset, the prime minister usually serves for four years, but his or her term may be shortened by a no-confidence vote in the Knesset.

Have You Heard of David Ben-Gurion? (1886-1973)

David Ben-Gurion was born in Poland and spent his childhood years studying in a religious school. He immigrated to Palestine in 1906 at the age of twenty. After briefly serving in the Russian army, he returned to Palestine during World War I and was exiled by the Ottomans for engaging in anti-Turkish activities. In 1915, he moved to New York and met and married a woman named Paula Munweis. In 1918, he joined the Jewish Legion of the British army. After World War I, he returned to Palestine with his family, and by 1930 he had become the leader of the dominant political party there. He also became the chairman of the Jewish Agency Executive, where, together with Chaim Weizmann, he directed all Zionist affairs of the Jewish Agency.

Ben-Gurion's decision to declare independence immediately after the expiration of the British Mandate was opposed by the US government and numerous Zionist leaders. After independence, Ben-Gurion became Israel's first prime minister, serving until he resigned in 1953.

A year later, prompted by the threat of war from the Arab states, the ruling party asked him to return to the government. He was appointed defense minister and eventually replaced Moshe Sharett as prime minister. Ben-Gurion resigned as prime minister in June 1963 and from the Knesset in 1970, retiring to Kibbutz Sde Boker in the Negev.

Forming Governments

In theory, the political party that wins the majority of seats in the Knesset chooses the prime minister, who then assigns cabinet positions. The prime minister and cabinet officials are often labeled "the government" while they are in power. In practice, though, no one political party has ever succeeded in winning a majority of the vote in Israel, so the party that wins the most votes is given the opportunity to form a coalition—or alliance—with other political parties; that coalition will then choose the prime minister. Because of this, Israeli governments have always been composed of coalitions of parties with often conflicting ideologies and agendas.

Prime ministers and their governments can only stay in power if they have the support of the majority of the Knesset. If at any time a sufficient number of Knesset members disagree with the government, they can vote to have new elections. Consequently, prime ministers need to satisfy the needs of their coalition partners, which has allowed smaller political parties in the country to exert great

STRAIGHT from the Source

In 1952, after Israel's first president, Chaim Weizmann, died, Albert Einstein was asked to be president of Israel. He declined but said:

"I am deeply moved by the offer from our State of Israel, and at once saddened and ashamed that I cannot accept it. All my life I have dealt with objective matters, hence I lack both the natural aptitude and the experience to deal properly with people and to exercise official functions. For these reasons alone I should be unsuited to fulfill the duties of that high office, even if advancing age was not making increasing inroads on my strength. I am the more distressed over these circumstances because my relationship to the Jewish people has become my strongest human bond, ever since I became fully aware of our precarious situation among the nations of the world."

influence on the government. For example, Israeli governments often have included members of religious parties who try to chip away at the separation that exists between religion and state, even while the secular parties push in the opposite direction, hoping to reduce the role of religion in public affairs.

Two Dominant Parties

Two parties have dominated Israeli politics over the years: the Labor Party, which has roots in Socialist Zionism, and the Likud Party and its predecessors, which grew out of the Revisionist Zionist tradition. Labor is considered more liberal on social issues and more open in its approach to security issues. Likud, which won its first election in 1977, is more conservative on domestic policy and typically more cautious on matters of national security. In 2005, the Likud split, and a new party called Kadima was created that attracted several Labor Party members and other centrists; Kadima then won the elections in March 2006. In March 2009, Likud returned to power, despite the fact that Kadima won one more seat in the Knesset, because it was able to build a broader coalition that gave it an overall majority.

As the number of Jews from the former Soviet Union has increased over the past two decades, a party representing their interests also has become more powerful. In addition, religious Jews have formed their own parties, and several Israeli Arab parties are represented in the Knesset. Because the Labor and Likud parties have a long history of animosity toward each other, they frequently choose to

Word Work

Labor Party The *Labor Party* was formed in Israel by the union of three left-of-center socialist parties. Labor (under different names) held power from 1948 until 1977, dominating Israeli public and political life. The party continues to be one of the major political parties in Israel.

Likud Party The *Likud Party* is the political party whose roots can be traced back to Vladimir Jabotinsky; it is associated with conservative, nationalist, free-market policies.

include religious parties and other small parties in their coalitions rather than work with one another. In 2009, however, Labor decided to align with the new Likud government headed by Benjamin Netanyahu, while Kadima became the leading opposition party.

LAW OF RETURN

Perhaps the most important piece of legislation adopted by the first Knesset in 1950 was the Law of Return, which provides Jews all over the world the right to immigrate to Israel and immediately become citizens if they choose to do so. This law legally recognizes the connection between the Jewish people and their homeland and considers every Jew settling in Israel a returning citizen.

This law changed the face of Israel and provided a lifeline to millions of Jews all over the world, allowing them to flee violence in their countries and settle in Israel. Prior to 1948, Jews had no haven, and they had learned through the catas-

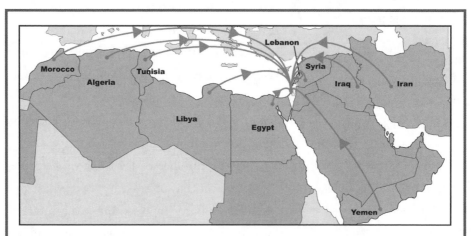

Between 1948 and 1972, thousands of Jews living in Arab states sought refuge in Israel. Included in this migration were 260,000 from Morocco, 14,000 from Algeria, 56,000 from Tunisia, 35,666 from Libya, 89,525 from Egypt, 6,000 from Lebanon, 4,500 from Syria, 129,290 from Iraq, and 50,552 from Yemen / Aden.

trophe of the Holocaust that they could not depend on other nations to protect them in times of trouble.

In 1947, as a showdown over partition approached in the United Nations, threats against Jews turned to violence in many Arab countries. More than a thousand Jews were killed in anti-Jewish rioting during the 1940s in Iraq, Libya, Egypt, Syria, and Yemen. This helped trigger a mass exodus of Jews from Arab countries, where they had lived for twenty-five hundred years.

> My greatest wish for Israel is that someday the citizens of Israel won't have to live in fear of tomorrow and Jews everywhere will have a place to call home.
>
> SAMANTHA, AGE 16,
> POTOMAC, MARYLAND

From 1949 to 1951, 104,000 Jews were evacuated from Iraq in Operation Ezra and Nehemiah; another 20,000 were smuggled out through Iran. Between 1949 and 1950, Operation Magic Carpet brought virtu-

STRAIGHT from the Source

"The Law of Return is one of the Basic Laws of the State of Israel. It comprises the central mission of our state, namely, ingathering of exiles. This law determines that it is not the state that grants the Jew from abroad the right to settle in the state. Rather, this right is inherent to him by the very fact that he is a Jew, if only he desires to join in the settlement of the land. In the State of Israel the Jews have no right of priority over the non-Jewish citizens. The State of Israel is grounded on the full equality of rights and obligations for all its citizens. This principle was also laid down in the Proclamation of Independence. The right to return preceded the State of Israel, and it is this right that built the state. This right originates in the unbroken historical connection between the people and the homeland."

—FROM AN ADDRESS BY DAVID BEN-GURION TO THE KNESSET, JULY 3, 1950

ally the entire Yemenite Jewish community—almost 50,000—to Israel. By 1951, immigrants had more than doubled the 1949 Jewish population of Israel, with the largest number coming from Morocco.

In recent years, the largest number of immigrants to Israel has come from the former Soviet Union. For decades Jews had tried to escape the totalitarian government there, but only handfuls were allowed to leave. As the Soviet Union began to dissolve in the late 1980s, the gates were finally opened, and the trickle of immigrants to Israel became a flood. Since 1990, more than one million Jews have emigrated from the countries of the former Soviet Union to Israel. For a nation the size of Israel to accept that many people is like the United States absorbing the entire population of France.

Although it did not represent as many people, a more dramatic operation was the rescue of the ancient Jewish community of Ethiopia. In spectacular airlifts in 1984 (Operation Moses), 1985 (Operation Joshua), and 1991 (Operation Solomon), Israel brought more than 20,000 Jews from Ethiopia back to their homeland. "For the first time in history," William Safire wrote in the *New York Times*, "thousands of black people are being brought into a country not in chains but as citizens."

Faces of Israel

Tikva, sixteen, lives in Hadera, a town on the Mediterranean coast between Tel Aviv and Haifa. Tikva's six older brothers and sisters were born in Ethiopia, so she is the first member of her family to be born in Israel. Her family came to Israel during Operation Moses in 1984, when Israel airlifted almost eight thousand Ethiopian Jews to Israel.

Tikva enjoys singing and is a member of a choir that practices twice a week. She hopes to travel abroad with her choir and to produce her own record featuring ancient Ethiopian melodies her family taught her.

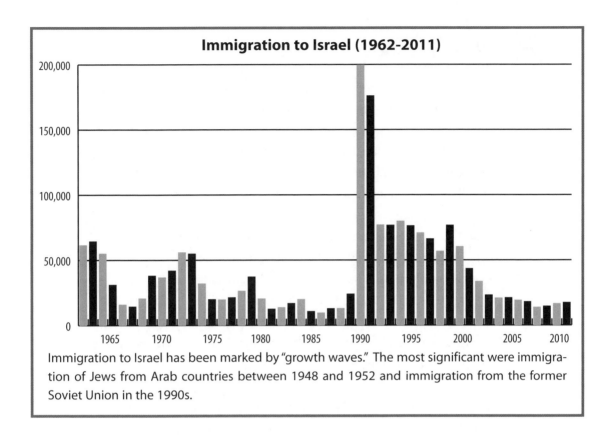

Immigration to Israel (1962-2011)

Immigration to Israel has been marked by "growth waves." The most significant were immigration of Jews from Arab countries between 1948 and 1952 and immigration from the former Soviet Union in the 1990s.

Although Jews in Western countries have the right to move to Israel, fewer have chosen to make *aliyah*, in comparison to Jews from other countries. While whole Jewish communities left Eastern European and Arab countries, fewer than one hundred thousand American Jews have moved to Israel in the past sixty years.

MINORITY RIGHTS

All people have equal rights in Israel according to the law, but in practice, many minorities struggle with discrimination in areas of housing, employment opportunities, and education. Israeli Arabs have equal voting rights, and Arabic, like Hebrew, is an official language in Israel. Israeli Arabs have formed their own political parties and have served in the Cabinet, in the foreign service, and on the

Word Work

Bedouin *Bedouin* are a minority within the Arab minority. Approximately 170,000 Bedouin live in Israel, most in the Negev desert. Formerly nomadic shepherds, the Bedouin are a tribal people that Israel is trying to integrate into the labor force and society. Some Bedouin remain committed to their traditional way of life, while others are making the transition to a permanently settled society.

Druze *Druze* are members of a Muslim sect that live primarily in Lebanon, southern Syria, and northern Israel. The basis of the Druze religion is the belief that God has been divinely incarnated in a living person and that his last, and final, such incarnation was al-Hakim, the sixth Fatimid caliph, who announced himself in Cairo about 1016 as the earthly incarnation of God. The Druze believe in one God, but they don't pray in a mosque and are secretive about the tenets of their religion.

Sunnis *Sunnis* are the largest group of Muslims worldwide. Sunnis accept the Islamic tradition and the legitimate authority of the caliphs as Muhammad's successors. Most Palestinian Muslims are Sunnis.

Supreme Court. There have even been Arab representatives in the Knesset who support Israel's enemies.

Muslims, Christians, Druze, Baha'is, Circassians, and other ethnic and religious groups represent more than 20 percent of Israel's population. The total population of Israel on the Jewish New Year in 2011 was 7.8 million. Just over 75 percent of the population is Jewish, and a little over 20 percent are Israeli Arabs. About 16 percent of the citizens are Muslims, two percent are Christians, and just under two percent are Druze. Israel is the only place in the Middle East where the Christian population has been growing.

Israel's diversity is also reflected in its educational system. There are secular schools, as well as special schools for Orthodox Jews and ultra-Orthodox (*Haredi*) Jews. There are schools for Arabs, where classes are taught in Arabic and more attention is paid to Arab history and Muslim traditions. Jewish schools, in which courses are taught in Hebrew, place greater emphasis on Jewish history and tradition. In recent years, more mixed schools have opened to promote better relations between Jews and people of other faiths. Many parents who want their children to interact with a more diverse student population have gravitated to these schools. At the college level, Arab students attend universities with Israeli Jews.

Most Israeli Arabs are exempt from military service. This exemption was adopted because of security concerns and to lessen the chances that an Israeli Arab would have to fight a relative from a neighboring country or territory.

Think about It

What challenges might occur when Jews from all over the world become citizens of one country? What are the benefits?

???

Word Work

Haredi In Israel, there are different forms of Orthodox Judaism. The word *Haredi* usually refers to Jews who observe a strict interpretation of the laws of Judaism and prefer to live in communities of like-minded Jews separated from other Israelis. Factions within this community do not support the state and believe the Messiah must come before a Jewish state can be created. Orthodox or Modern Orthodox Jews consider their interpretation of the Jewish law to be strict but are more willing to live among their fellow non-Orthodox Jews. The growing Masorti movement is affiliated with the Conservative movement in America, while the Progressive movement is affiliated with Reform. And many Israeli Jews are secular, yet still observe Jewish holidays and adhere to many Jewish practices.

Faces of Israel

Leonid, seventeen, arrived in Israel from Vladivostok when he was seven years old. He has few memories of Russia but knows his family suffered there because they were Jewish. They wanted to come to Israel but couldn't for many years because of Soviet restrictions on emigration.

Both of Leonid's parents are mathematicians and were university professors in Russia. After living in trailers for two years in Israel, the family settled in Tel Aviv, where Leonid's parents both teach school.

Leonid plays the piano and already performs publicly at different local venues. After his military service, he hopes to enter Tel Aviv's Academy of Music. Along with his love for music, Leonid also plays chess and enjoys Tel Aviv's nightlife.

Druze and Circassians, also Muslim communities, do serve, and Bedouin and other Arabs have volunteered for military duty.

Israeli Arabs and other Israelis are outspoken about issues of social inequality, such as government funding for Israeli Arab municipalities and schools. Israel's leaders face the ongoing challenge of balancing the rights and needs of people from dozens of religious and ethnic groups and immigrants from around the globe.

CHAPTER EIGHT

THE CHALLENGE OF TERRITORY

After winning decisive victories against its Arab foes in 1948, Israel expected its neighbors to accept its independence as a fact and negotiate peace. But this did not happen. Even though it had signed an armistice agreement with Israel in 1949, Egypt was not willing to make a permanent peace with Israel; to the contrary, it began preparing for war.

First, Egyptian president Gamal Abdel Nasser, who took power in 1954, kept the Suez Canal closed to Israeli shipping, violating the agreement Israel

Word Work

terrorism *Terrorism* is defined by the FBI as "the unlawful use of force or violence against persons or property to intimidate or coerce a government, the civilian population, or any segment thereof, in furtherance of political or social objectives."

and Egypt had signed after the war. He then began to import arms from the Soviet bloc, building an arsenal for a confrontation with Israel.

Nasser's arms deals were part of an ongoing competition in the region between the United States and the Soviet Union. The Communists in the Soviet Union hoped to spread their ideology throughout the Middle East and gain control of the oil in the region. The United States generally responded by supporting regimes that opposed the Soviet Union. Both sides tried to gain influence in a variety of ways, particularly by arming their allies, sparking an arms race that added to the tension in the region and sometimes threatened to boil over into a direct conflict between the two superpowers.

While Nasser built his arsenal, he also began to send Palestinian terrorists called fedayeen ("those who sacrifice themselves") from Gaza to infiltrate Israel to commit acts of sabotage and murder. He also ratcheted up the pressure on Israel by creating an Egyptian blockade of the Straits of Tiran, Israel's only supply route with Africa and Asia in the south of the country. Then Nasser nationalized the Suez Canal, which had been owned by British and French stockholders.

ISRAEL RESPONDS

From Israel's perspective, the blockades, combined with increased terrorist attacks and threatening Egyptian statements, made the situation intolerable. Rather than wait for Nasser and his allies to build up their forces sufficiently to wage a new war, Israeli prime minister David Ben-Gurion decided to launch a preemptive strike. He devised a plan with the British and French, who hoped to regain control of the Suez Canal, and the three nations attacked Egypt at the end of October 1956. In only one hundred hours of fighting, Israel captured most of the Sinai desert and the Gaza Strip from Egypt.

Have You Heard of Gamal Abdel Nasser? (1918–1970)

Gamal Abdel Nasser was born in Alexandria on January 15, 1918. He attended a military academy and later served in the Egyptian army, where he became friendly with a group of officers who created a secret revolutionary society, the Free Officers. These officers wanted to end British influence in Egypt and overthrow the Egyptian king.

In 1952, the Free Officers staged a coup and ousted King Farouk. Two years later, Nasser seized control of the government; he was officially elected president in 1956. In that year, Egypt provoked the Europeans by nationalizing the Suez Canal and threatened Israel by sponsoring terrorist attacks against it. In response, Israel, Britain, and France attacked Egypt.

Even though he lost the Suez War, Nasser's willingness to stand up to the Western powers, including the United States, made him a hero to many. He was especially popular in Arab nations because he promoted the idea of uniting the Arab world, a philosophy called pan-Arabism.

Eleven years later, after Egypt's defeat in the 1967 Six-Day War, Nasser resigned. But public support for him was so high that he withdrew his resignation and remained president. His image had been tarnished, however, by Egypt's losses in that war, and he never regained his previous stature. He suffered a heart attack and died in office on September 28, 1970.

US president Dwight Eisenhower was infuriated that Britain, France, and Israel had ignored American appeals not to go to war and did not tell the United States of their intentions. Eisenhower was especially angry at Israel and threatened

Word Work

Palestine Liberation Organization The *Palestine Liberation Organization* is comprised of several groups. Fatah is the dominant faction; the PLO also includes the Popular Front for the Liberation of Palestine and the Democratic Front for the Liberation of Palestine. The PLO was formed at the Cairo Summit of 1964. It was originally controlled by the Arab states, but after the Six-Day War the Palestinians themselves took control of the organization, which was led by Yasser Arafat until his death in 2004. The PLO's stated goal was the "liberation of Palestine," and it used terrorism as a means to advance that goal. In 1993, Arafat renounced the use of violence, which was the catalyst for subsequent peace talks with Israel, but those ultimately failed in large measure because the PLO continued to engage in terror.

to discontinue all US government assistance, impose UN sanctions, and end all private contributions to Israel if it didn't withdraw from the areas it had conquered. Ben-Gurion bowed to the pressure and pulled out of the Sinai, even though Egypt had not agreed to live in peace with Israel.

Israel did receive assurances from the United States, however, that it would keep its shipping lanes open to Israel, and a UN Emergency Force was established and deployed on the border between Egypt and Israel to help prevent future attacks.

SIX DAYS THAT SHOCKED THE WORLD

In 1964, Egypt and other Arab nations established the Palestine Liberation Organization (PLO) as a new weapon in the war against Israel. The PLO launched numerous terrorist attacks against Israelis and became the umbrella group of a number of Palestinian factions that had a common interest in destroying Israel.

Meanwhile, the Syrian army used the Golan Heights, a mountainous region towering approximately three thousand feet above the Galilee in northern Israel, to shell Israeli farms and villages. Syria's attacks grew more frequent in 1965 and 1966, forcing families living on *kibbutzim* in the valley below the heights to sleep in bomb shelters.

In May 1967, Nasser ordered the withdrawal of the UN Emergency Force that had been

STRAIGHT from the **Source**

"The Balfour Declaration, the Mandate for Palestine, and everything that has been based upon them, are deemed null and void. Claims of historical or religious ties of Jews with Palestine are incompatible with the facts of history and the true conception of what constitutes statehood. Judaism, being a religion, is not an independent nationality. Nor do Jews constitute a single nation with an identity of its own; they are citizens of the states to which they belong."

— ARTICLE 20 FROM THE PLO CHARTER DENYING JEWS HAVE THE RIGHT TO SELF-DETERMINATION

stationed in the Sinai after the 1956 war and again closed the Straits of Tiran to all Israeli shipping and all ships bound for Eilat, Israel's southernmost port. As the world watched, Arab armies began to encircle Israel as Arab leaders called for the Jewish state's destruction and promised an imminent attack.

Israel Attacks

Israel was at enormous risk: if it did nothing and waited for the attack Nasser and other Arab leaders promised was coming, Israel would be at a potentially catastrophic military disadvantage. So Israeli leaders planned a surprise attack. On June 5, 1967, the order was given to attack Egypt, the most powerful Arab country, whose leader had precipitated the crisis.

That same day, Israeli prime minister Levi Eshkol sent a message to King Hussein of Jordan, promising him that Israel would not fight Jordan unless Hussein attacked Israel first. The Jordanian king ignored the Israeli overture and attacked, as he was unable to withstand pressure from his Arab neighbors to join a war with the Jewish state. Israel fought back.

STRAIGHT from the **Source**

"Our basic objective will be the destruction of Israel. The Arab people want to fight."

–PRESIDENT GAMAL ABDEL NASSER, MAY 27, 1967

Word Work

West Bank The *West Bank* refers to the land west of the Jordan River that the Israelis captured from Jordan in 1967. This area includes the territories that were known as Judea and Samaria in biblical times and was the region where Jews actually lived in that period.

The Golan Heights, the West Bank, and the Sinai Peninsula were captured by Israel during the Six-Day War.

Within a few hours, the Israeli air force destroyed nearly the entire Egyptian and Jordanian air forces and half of Syria's air force while their planes were still on the ground. After just six days of fighting, Israeli forces broke through enemy lines and were in a position to march on the Arab capitals of Cairo, Egypt; Damascus, Syria; and Amman, Jordan.

By this time, the principal objectives of capturing the Sinai and the Golan Heights had been accomplished. In addition, while battling Jordanian forces, Israel had captured the eastern half of Jerusalem, including the Old City, and the West Bank, which Jordan had occupied ever since the 1948 War of Independence. Just six days after their surprise attack began, Israel agreed to end the fighting.

Although it lasted only a few days—and came to be known as the Six-Day War—the death toll for Israel was high: about 770 soldiers were killed in the war.

Israel Gains Respect and Arabs Remain Defiant

The Six-Day War had a tremendous impact on the nations of the region and how they were perceived by the international community. Much of the world was

Have You Heard of King Hussein bin Talal? (1935-1999)

HIS MAJESTY K?
OF THE HA?

Prior to his death in 1999, King Hussein bin Talal of Jordan was the longest serving executive head of state in the world. He was born in Amman on November 14, 1935, and, after completing his elementary education there, attended Victoria College in Alexandria, Egypt, and Harrow School in England. He later received his military education at the Royal Military Academy Sandhurst in England.

In 1951, Hussein witnessed the assassination of his grandfather, King Abdullah, at the Al-Aqsa Mosque in Jerusalem. (Most experts believe Abdullah was assassinated by a Palestinian who was critical of his tolerance of Israel.) Hussein's father, King Talal, who was Abdullah's oldest son, assumed the throne, but he was found to be mentally incapacitated. When he was eighteen years old, Hussein was proclaimed king.

Hussein came to be considered a political moderate with close ties to the United States. But in 1967, fearful of his Arab neighbors, he decided to attack Israel and subsequently lost control of East Jerusalem and the West Bank, territories his grandfather had conquered in the 1948 War of Independence.

Afterward, he frequently engaged in secret negotiations with Israel but was not prepared to finalize a peace agreement until 1994, after Palestinians had signed their own agreement with Israel.

King Hussein died of cancer in early 1999 and was succeeded by his oldest son, Abdullah.

Think about It

What factors led to Israel's decision to attack Egypt in 1967?

???

impressed with Israel's military prowess. Israel was viewed as David defeating the Arab Goliath.

This newfound respect and admiration for Israel was in sharp contrast to the devastation expressed by the leaders of the Arab nations. Many Muslims expressed surprise that the Jews could defeat them. These emotional reactions to the outcome of the war shaped how both sides behaved in its aftermath.

Israeli leaders expected the decisive victory to convince the Arab leadership that Israel could not be defeated militarily, and they assumed the Arabs would be open to negotiating a peace settlement. Israeli leaders even expressed their willingness to give up the territory it had just won in exchange for a guarantee of peace. But the Arab leaders were not willing to make concessions.

Rather than respond positively to Israel's peace overture, the Arab nations reacted defiantly. At a meeting in Khartoum, Sudan, in August 1967, Arab leaders offered the declaration that has become known as the Three Nos: "No peace with Israel, no negotiations with Israel, no recognition of Israel."

The United Nation Responds

Part of the Arab strategy was to try to use the United Nations to gain diplomatically what they could not achieve militarily. When the UN Security Council on November 22, 1967, unanimously passed Resolution 242 to provide guidelines for a peace settlement, the Arab states chose to interpret the initiative selectively, so that all the responsibility for concessions was placed on the Israelis and none on themselves.

The resolution clearly anticipated that the Arab states would make peace with Israel, while also saying that Israel should withdraw from "territories occupied" in 1967. However, the Security Council did not require Israel to withdraw from *all* the territories occupied after the Six-Day War. This wording was quite deliberate and reflected the resolution drafters' view that Israel must withdraw from some, but not necessarily all, of the territories it captured—in exchange for peace.

STRAIGHT from the Source

"The Security Council,

Expressing its continuing concern with the grave situation in the Middle East,

Emphasizing the inadmissibility of the acquisition of territory by war and the need to work for a just and lasting peace in which every State in the area can live in security,

Emphasizing further that all Member States in their acceptance of the Charter of the United Nations have undertaken a commitment to act in accordance with Article 2 of the Charter,

1. Affirms that the fulfillment of Charter principles requires the establishment of a just and lasting peace in the Middle East which should include the application of both the following principles:

    (i) Withdrawal of Israel armed forces from territories occupied in the recent conflict;

    (ii) Termination of all claims or states of belligerency and respect for and acknowledgment of the sovereignty, territorial integrity and political independence of every State in the area and their right to live in peace within secure and recognized boundaries free from threats or acts of force;

2. Affirms further the necessity:

    (a) For guaranteeing freedom of navigation through international waterways in the area;

    (b) For achieving a just settlement of the refugee problem;

    (c) For guaranteeing the territorial inviolability and political independence of every State in the area, through measures including the establishment of demilitarized zones;

3. Requests the Secretary-General to designate a Special Representative to proceed to the Middle East to establish and maintain contacts with the States concerned in order to promote agreement and assist efforts to achieve a peaceful and accepted settlement in accordance with the provisions and principles in this resolution;

4. Requests the Secretary-General to report to the Security Council on the progress of the efforts of the Special Representative as soon as possible."

—UN Security Council Resolution 242

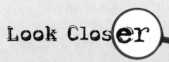

Look Closer

Although UN Security Council Resolution 242 is viewed as the basis for negotiations between Israel and the Palestinians, the Palestinians are not mentioned anywhere in the text.

The Security Council members understood that Israel's previous borders had been indefensible and that some adjustments were needed. However, the Arab states objected to the call for "secure and recognized boundaries" because they feared that this wording implied an acceptance of Israel.

Israel Holds On to Land

Because the Arabs would not negotiate with Israel, even following the UN Resolution, Israel chose to hold on to the West Bank, which it had captured from Jordan; the Golan Heights, which it won from Syria; and the Gaza Strip and Sinai Peninsula, which were taken from Egypt, until some or all of these lands could be exchanged as part of a peace agreement.

Holding on to the Golan Heights and Sinai also gave Israel military advantages. Instead of the Syrians looking down on Israel from the Golan, the Israelis now had the high ground from which to monitor the Syrians. In the south, the Sinai provided a huge, sparsely populated desert that separated the Israeli population from Egypt.

In the West Bank and Gaza, Israel gained some strategically valuable space, but those territories were also home to millions of Palestinians, and Israel now became responsible for their well-being. While Israel took measures to improve living conditions in the West Bank and Gaza, such as building schools and providing health care, the overall living conditions in the area were substandard. Israel also needed to impose security restrictions on the Palestinians to ensure that no terrorists could infiltrate Israel.

PALESTINIANS STEP UP RESPONSES

Because Israel never formally annexed the West Bank outside of Jerusalem, the Palestinians living there did not become Israeli citizens and did not have the same rights as the country's Arab citizens. The Palestinians in the West Bank consequently faced hardships; these difficulties, combined with the imposition of periodic curfews and the establishment of security checkpoints, embittered many Palestinians and provoked some to join terrorist groups.

Before the Six-Day War, Palestinians had engaged in some terrorist attacks against Israel but had primarily counted on the neighboring Arab states to conquer Israel and win back their homes. After the Six-Day War, however, many Palestinians began to believe they could not rely on the Arab states to destroy Israel, so they began to try harder to do it themselves. The Palestinians had made no effort to establish a Palestinian state in the West Bank during the nineteen years it had been controlled by Jordan, or in the Gaza Strip while it was under Egyptian occupation. But now that Israel was governing those regions, the Palestinians began to push for independence in those territories.

In an attempt to gain international attention, the PLO and other organizations engaged in spectacular terrorist attacks, such as hijacking civilian airplanes and setting off bombs in public places. There were more than thirteen major Palestinian terrorist attacks between the 1967 and 1973 wars, including the 1968 hijacking of an El Al flight from Rome, Italy; an attack on a school bus in Avivim, Israel, in 1970 that resulted in twelve deaths, including nine children; and the murder of eleven members of the Israeli Olympic team in Munich, Germany, in 1972.

The Palestinians were further enraged when Israel began to allow Jews to move into the West Bank and Gaza Strip. Initially, Israel's primary interest was to create strategic outposts in key locations to prevent possible future invasions. Later, Jews began to move to areas such as Hebron and Kfar Etzion, resettling in communities where they had lived before being driven out by the Arabs. While some were motivated by ideological or religious fervor, other Israelis settled there for economic reasons (the

Think about It

Why were the United States and the Soviet Union involved in the Middle East conflict? What interests did each country have in the region?

Look Closer

In May 1948, residents of four *kibbutzim* just outside Jerusalem, in an area called Gush Etzion, held off a large Arab army headed for Jerusalem. The Jordanian Legion, backed by thousands of local Arabs, killed 240 residents of the *kibbutzim*; another 260 were captured, and the settlements were razed. In 1967, descendants of the Jews who fought and died in one kibbutz, Kfar Etzion, established the first community in the West Bank in the area of the original farms. This and other Jewish communities established in the West Bank and Gaza Strip are typically referred to as "settlements."

government subsidized housing in the territories, and it was possible to get a nice home in close proximity to major cities and jobs).

As more Jews built communities in the West Bank, the Palestinians grew increasingly bitter and worried about whether Israel would ever withdraw or allow the creation of a Palestinian state. Even so, many never gave up hope that Israel would ultimately disappear from the entire region.

Think about It

What prevented the Arab states and Israel from negotiating a peace agreement following the Six-Day War?

???

CHAPTER NINE

A BIT OF PEACE, MORE BATTLES

After the Six-Day War, Israel's leaders expected to negotiate agreements with neighboring Arab states that would involve giving up some of Israel's conquered territory in exchange for promises of security. Rather than moving closer to peace, however, Egyptian president Nasser resumed fighting.

He believed that because most of Israel's army consisted of reserves, the country could not withstand a lengthy war or endure the economic burden caused when citizens had to leave their jobs to fight. Nasser also hoped that a steady stream of casualties would undermine Israeli morale and that, if the situation became dangerous enough, the United States would pressure Israel to withdraw from the captured territories. Consequently, from March 1969 until August 1970, Egypt engaged in persistent attacks against Israel, shelling Israeli positions along the Suez Canal, which led to a gradual escalation of hostilities between the two sides.

The leaders of the United States became alarmed by the fighting and by the Soviet Union's close cooperation with Egypt, as well as the threats it was issuing against Israel. President Richard Nixon and Secretary of State Henry Kissinger viewed the situation as a challenge to US interests and made an all-out effort to convince Egypt and Israel to accept a ceasefire, which they did on August 7, 1970. Although this "War of Attrition" has been largely forgotten, the Israeli death toll was 1,424 soldiers and more than 100 civilians—almost twice as many casualties as in the Six-Day War.

Nasser had been correct when he predicted that a war of attrition would sap Israeli morale. While Israelis had enjoyed a sense of euphoria over its dramatic victory in 1967, their confidence had suffered under Egypt's persistent shelling and Palestinian terrorist attacks. Peace seemed farther away than ever after the surge of terrorism that culminated in the murder of eleven Israeli athletes by Palestinian terrorists at the 1972 Munich Olympics. War was once again on the horizon.

THE YOM KIPPUR WAR

On October 6, 1973, Egypt and Syria launched a surprise attack against Israel on Yom Kippur, the holiest day of the Jewish calendar. On the Golan Heights, approximately 180 Israeli tanks faced an onslaught of 1,400 Syrian tanks. Along the Suez Canal, fewer than 500 Israeli defenders with three tanks were attacked by 600,000 Egyptian soldiers, backed by 2,000 tanks and 550 aircraft.

Thrown on the defensive during the first two days of fighting, Israel mobilized its reserves and began to counterattack. As Israel's situation grew more pre-

Look Closer

At 4:30 a.m. on September 5, 1972, five Arab terrorists wearing track suits climbed the six-and-a-half-foot fence surrounding the Olympic Village, where the athletes were staying, and were met by three more men inside. The Palestinians then used stolen keys to enter two apartments being used by the Israeli Olympic team.

Wrestling coach Moshe Weinberg and weightlifter Yossef Romano were killed while fighting the attackers, who succeeded in rounding up nine Israelis to hold as hostages. The terrorists, part of a Palestinian Liberation Organization group called Black September, demanded that Israel release two hundred Arab prisoners and give them safe passage out of Germany.

As the whole world watched the drama unfold, the terrorists agreed to be taken by helicopter to a NATO air base, where they were told they would receive an airplane to fly to Cairo. At the airport, German police attempted to kill the terrorists, and a bloody firefight ensued. Around 11:00 p.m., the media was mistakenly informed that the hostages had been saved. Almost an hour later, however, new fighting broke out and one of the helicopters holding the Israelis was blown up by a terrorist grenade. The remaining hostages in the second helicopter were shot to death by one of the surviving terrorists.

At 3:00 a.m. in Germany, US television reporter Jim McKay, who had been bringing the story to Americans all day as part of ABC's Olympic coverage, announced: "They're all gone."

Five of the terrorists were killed along with one policeman; three terrorists were captured but were released a little more than a month later in order to meet the demands of a separate group of terrorists who had hijacked a Lufthansa jet.

Have You Heard of Golda Meir? (1898–1978)

Golda Mabovitch was born in Kiev, in the Russian Empire (today Ukraine), and raised in Milwaukee, Wisconsin. In 1917, she married Morris Meyerson, and, in 1921, they settled in Palestine on Kibbutz Merhavia and Hebraized their surname name to Meir, which means to "burn brightly."

In 1924, Golda Meir became active in the Histadrut, the Jewish trade union, and became increasingly involved in Zionist politics. After World War II, she became the chief Jewish liaison with the British and later raised money in the United States to fund Israel's War of Independence. David Ben-Gurion also appointed her to his provisional government and dispatched Meir for secret meetings with Jordan's King Abdullah in the hope of averting war. These meetings failed.

Following independence, Meir was appointed Israel's ambassador to the Soviet Union; she was later elected to the Knesset as a member of Mapai (the Labor Party at that time). In 1956, she began a nearly ten-year tenure as foreign minister, during which she built strong ties between Israel and the developing world, especially Africa.

Upon Levi Eshkol's death in 1969, Meir became prime minister at age 71, the world's third female prime minister. The major event of her administration was the Yom Kippur War. Many Israelis, and a commission of inquiry, blamed Meir for failing to be prepared for the attack. Meir was still reelected shortly after the war but felt responsible for the government's failure and resigned in 1974. She passed away in December 1978 and was buried on Mount Herzl in Jerusalem.

What Would YOU Do?

You are sitting in the prime minister's office on October 5, 1973. Israel's top intelligence officials indicate alarming troop movements by Egypt and Syria, but they do not believe a war is imminent. Early the next morning, you are called back to meet with Prime Minister Golda Meir. General David Elazar, the chief of staff, is recommending that all Israeli forces be mobilized immediately and that the air force launch a preemptive attack.

Meir has informed US secretary of state Henry Kissinger that she is concerned about the possibility of war, but Kissinger tells her Israel should not shoot first. You know Israel's chances for victory and minimizing casualties will be better if Meir orders a preemptive strike and the rapid mobilization of the IDF. Striking first, however, after Kissinger's warning, might upset the leaders of the United States, and President Nixon may not support Israel during the war or its policies afterward.

What would you advise the prime minister to do?

What Really Happened

Prime Minister Meir ordered a partial call-up of reserves but didn't authorize a preemptive strike because she did not want to risk losing US support. Egypt and Syria attacked, and Israel suffered many casualties in the early days of the war.

carious, President Nixon ordered an emergency airlift of military supplies and weapons to Israel. Cargo planes carrying spare parts, tanks, bombs, and helicopters flew round-the-clock.

As the fighting against Syria and Egypt escalated, Israel began to push back the Arab attackers until it was able to threaten the Egyptian and Syrian capitals. At that point, the Soviet Union threatened to intervene in the fighting, and the

US government became concerned that the hostilities could escalate to a serious US-Soviet confrontation. When the Soviet Union pressed for an end to the fighting, Kissinger flew to Moscow, and the two sides agreed to the adoption of UN Security Council Resolution 338, which called for an immediate ceasefire.

The resolution ended the fighting, which Jews call the Yom Kippur War and Arabs refer to as the Ramadan War because it occurred during this Muslim holiday.

Word Work

OPEC *OPEC*—the Organization of the Petroleum Exporting Countries—was formed in 1960 by Iran, Iraq, Kuwait, Saudi Arabia, and Venezuela to try to control oil prices by restricting supply . The five founding members were later joined by Qatar, Indonesia, Libya, United Arab Emirates, Algeria, Nigeria, Ecuador, Angola, and Gabon. Today, OPEC continues to influence the price of oil by regulating the amount each country produces. However, its influence is blunted by the policies of other oil producers that are not part of OPEC, such as the United States, Mexico, Norway, and Russia.

Despite the army's ultimate success on the battlefield, the 1973 war was considered an Israeli diplomatic and intelligence failure. Israelis were horrified by the fact that the Arabs had succeeded in surprising the IDF and inflicting heavy losses—2,688 Israeli soldiers were killed—against the stronger Israeli army. Prime Minister Golda Meir accepted responsibility for the lack of preparation and resigned. Yitzhak Rabin, a former IDF chief of staff and Israeli ambassador to the United States, replaced her.

TARGETING AMERICA

The Arab oil-producing states announced an oil embargo against the United States on October 19, 1973, to protest America's support for Israel. Taking advantage of the embargo, world oil producers (Arab and non-Arab) declared substantial price hikes in oil and gasoline.

The action rocked world economies, leading to the rationing of gasoline and long lines at gas stations in the United States and other Western countries. The conflict between Israel and its Arab neighbors was now wreaking havoc on the everyday lives of people in the United States.

Look Closer

On June 27, 1976, four terrorists forced an Air France Airbus, flying from Israel to Paris via Athens, to land in Uganda and demanded that Israel release 53 convicted terrorists. The hijackers freed the French crew and non-Jewish passengers but held 105 Jewish and Israeli hostages and said they would begin executing them in 48 hours. The Israeli government announced it would enter into negotiations, buying time for the hostages while it was secretly preparing a rescue plan.

Late on July 3, an Israeli rescue force landed at the Ugandan airport in a cargo plane carrying two jeeps and a black Mercedes, which was a perfect copy of Ugandan dictator Idi Amin's personal car. Two additional planes carried reinforcements and troops assigned to carry out special missions, such as destroying Ugandan air force jets parked nearby. A fourth plane was sent to evacuate the hostages.

Lt. Col. Yonatan Netanyahu led a lightning raid. All eight terrorists were killed, and two hostages died when they were caught in the crossfire. Netanyahu was killed as he led the hostages toward the safety of the Israeli planes.

News of the dramatic victory against terrorism at Uganda's Entebbe airport was announced on July 4, 1976, as the United States celebrated its bicentennial. The spectacular rescue impressed the world and lifted the morale of Israelis, demonstrating that Israel would take dramatic action to protect Jewish lives.

After the Arab states failed to defeat Israel, Palestinians once again turned to violence and targeted Israelis and Jews wherever they could. Terrorism became a growing threat around the world.

EGYPT NEGOTIATES WITH ISRAEL

Israel again hoped that by proving it could not be defeated militarily, Arab leaders would abandon their efforts to destroy Israel and seek to negotiate. Initially, the Arab states gave no indication they had changed their goals. Egyptian president Anwar Sadat, however, began to show an interest in changing his country's

Have You Heard of Menachem Begin? (1913–1992)

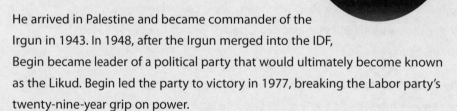

Menachem Begin was born in Brest-Litovsk, Poland, in 1913. He joined the revisionist Betar movement as a teenager and in 1938 became the leader of the movement in Poland. His Zionist activities resulted in a brief stay in a Russian prison camp in Siberia.

He arrived in Palestine and became commander of the Irgun in 1943. In 1948, after the Irgun merged into the IDF, Begin became leader of a political party that would ultimately become known as the Likud. Begin led the party to victory in 1977, breaking the Labor party's twenty-nine-year grip on power.

By signing the historic Camp David Peace Accords with Egypt, Begin became the first prime minister to make peace with an Arab neighbor. Begin also ordered the 1981 air strike that destroyed a nuclear reactor in Iraq and began rescue operations to bring Ethiopia's Jews to Israel in the early 1980s.

But Begin resigned as prime minister and left the public scene completely in 1983 as a result of his despair over the course of the Lebanon War and the death of his wife.

relationship with both Israel and the United States. A longtime Soviet ally, Sadat had expelled Soviet advisors from Egypt in 1972 and had seen during the 1973 war how American support for Israel was more beneficial than Soviet support for the Arabs. He subsequently decided to improve ties with the United States, which he knew also would require him to reduce tensions with Israel. Sadat believed that by surprising the Israelis in 1973 and nearly defeating them, Egypt had erased the shame of the 1967 rout. This made it possible for him to entertain for the first time the idea of pursuing peace with Israel and retrieving lost territory through negotiations rather than fighting. With the help of the shuttle diplomacy of US secretary of state Kissinger, Israel and Egypt negotiated agreements that led to an Israeli withdrawal from parts of the Sinai it had captured in 1973.

Menachem Begin was elected as Israel's first non-Labor Party prime minister in 1977. A member of the right-wing Herut Party, he had long been known for having led the Irgun underground during the 1940s and then advocating a vision of "Greater Israel," whereby Israel would eventually incorporate the Gaza Strip and the West Bank into the Jewish state. Because he was viewed as a "hard-liner," the people of Israel had faith that if Begin made a deal, he would ensure that Israel's security would be protected. Begin opened secret negotiations with Egypt and sought a deal with Sadat, whereby Israel would return part of the Sinai in exchange for peace with Egypt. Sadat made a bold gesture when he traveled to Jerusalem to address the Knesset, becoming the first Arab head of state to visit

Israel. Israelis were thrilled by Sadat's visit, which helped convince them that Sadat was prepared to make peace.

Even though all sides were interested in reaching a peace agreement, negotiations remained very difficult. Israel was asked to give up tangible possessions—land, oil fields, and military bases—while Egypt offered only the intangible, a promise not to attack Israel. The Egyptians and Israelis needed assistance to resolve their differences, and US president Jimmy Carter believed he could help, inviting Begin and Sadat to the presidential retreat at Camp David in September 1978. There Carter brokered two agreements that laid the foundation for the peace treaty that was signed on March 26, 1979.

Look Closer

Although most Israelis rejoiced at the signing of the peace treaty with Egypt, as the years passed, many grew disappointed that the treaty didn't lead to genuine friendship. In October 1981, Sadat was assassinated by Islamic extremists angry because he had made peace with Israel. His successor, Hosni Mubarak, visited Israel only once during his thirty years as president, for Yitzhak Rabin's funeral.

Most trade and tourism has been in one direction, from Israel to Egypt, and the state-controlled Egyptian media has often published and broadcast anti-Semitic material. Despite what Israelis refer to as the "cold peace" with Egypt, they are still satisfied to have the treaty. There has been no military conflict between Israel and Egypt since the treaty was signed. In 2011, however, a popular uprising in Egypt led to the overthrow of Mubarak and an uncertain future for Egypt's government. The military rulers who took immediate control of the government indicated they remained committed to peace with Israel, but many other Egyptians began to call for changes in the treaty or abrogating it altogether.

The agreements represented a monumental shift in Middle East relations. Begin had made startling concessions, agreeing to sacrifice the strategic depth of the desert and withdraw from the entire Sinai, with its settlements and military bases. He also was willing to grant the Palestinians a measure of autonomy. In return, Egypt agreed to exchange ambassadors, allow tourists to travel back and forth between the countries, and begin to openly trade with Israel. The treaty fulfilled the thirty-year dream of Israelis to achieve peace with their neighbor.

Think about It

Why did Egypt break with the rest of the Arab nations and negotiate peace with Israel?

? ? ?

Word Work

Judea/Samaria *Judea* and *Samaria* are names that have long been used for the regions west of the Jordan River. However, since Menachem Begin's time, these geographic references have acquired political meaning. People who refer to Judea and Samaria in political debate usually believe these territories are part of Israel and should remain so. Those who refer to the area simply as the West Bank are speaking in geographical terms. Discussions of the future of this disputed territory usually refer to it as the West Bank.

The Israeli government had hoped the breakthrough with Egypt would lead to a comprehensive peace with the rest of the Arab world; however, other Arab leaders refused to follow Sadat's example, instead ostracizing him and isolating Egypt. In fact, two years after signing the treaty, Sadat was assassinated by terrorists who objected to the Israeli peace deal. Meanwhile, the Palestinians rejected Begin's autonomy offer because it did not give them complete independence from Israeli rule, and Arafat was not yet prepared to recognize Israel's right to exist and give up the armed struggle to liberate all of Palestine.

DISPUTED SETTLEMENTS

A major sticking point in the discussions regarding Palestinian autonomy was the presence of Jewish settlements in the territories, especially the West Bank and the Gaza Strip.

Word Work

Green Line The *Green Line* was the armistice line between Israel and Jordan from 1949 until 1967. It now demarcates the boundary between pre-1967 Israel and the West Bank territories captured in the Six-Day War. The reference is believed to have come from Moshe Dayan drawing the armistice line on a map in green.

Begin opposed the creation of a Palestinian state and believed Jews had as much right to live in the West Bank, the area where Jews had been concentrated in the biblical period, as did Palestinians. In fact, Begin advocated expanding Jewish communities into the West Bank, at least in part to make the creation of a Palestinian state more difficult. Still, at the time the Palestinians rejected his autonomy offer, fewer than six thousand Jews lived in the territories.

Three different types of Jewish settlers lived in the West Bank. The original settlers who had established communities for security reasons had been joined by a second group of religious Zionists. This group moved into areas they believed had biblical significance, proclaiming

Faces of Israel

Abigail, sixteen, resides in Ofra, a Jewish settlement located between Jerusalem and the Palestinian town of Nablus. She is a second-generation resident of her small town, which was established in the mid-1970s.

Her family is observant, and her grandparents were the only members of their family to survive the Holocaust in Hungary. Like her older sister and two brothers, Abigail goes to a religious boarding school.

Like many Orthodox Jewish young women, she hopes to volunteer for two years of civil service in a home for the elderly instead of doing her military service. In the future, she plans to return to Ofra and work as a teacher.

them to be part of the land promised to the Jews, and therefore holy and belonging to Israel. Some of these communities were established in areas with large Palestinian populations, often creating tensions between Jews and Arabs. A third group of Jews began to create communities just beyond the pre-1967 borders, because the Israeli government offered them financial incentives to move to these areas. The offers were attractive because settlers could often find nicer houses at lower cost than those available inside the Green Line, and many of the communities were essentially suburbs of Jerusalem and close to the settlers' places of employment. Originally, the government wanted to encourage people to live in these areas for security reasons, but later, particularly after Begin came to power, the objective was to take control of greater swathes of territory to potentially annex territory and expand the state of Israel or to make it more difficult to establish a Palestinian state.

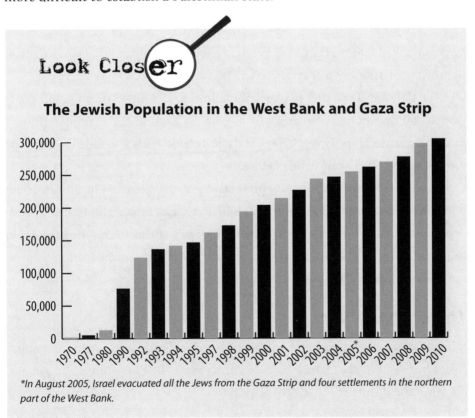

Look Closer

The Jewish Population in the West Bank and Gaza Strip

In August 2005, Israel evacuated all the Jews from the Gaza Strip and four settlements in the northern part of the West Bank.

The swelling Jewish settlement population angered the Palestinians, who considered the settlements a provocation. However, the Palestinians continued to reject any compromise with Israel and insisted on "liberating Palestine," by which they meant destroying all of Israel. The issue of building new settlements became hotly debated among Israelis.

THE GALILEE

Although Israelis hoped that peace with Egypt would encourage other nations to follow Sadat's example or at least bring a respite in its conflict with the Arabs, continuing violence along Israel's northern frontier soon engulfed the nation in its sixth war.

Israel had long sought a peaceful border with Lebanon, but that country's position as a haven for terrorist groups made this impossible. In 1978, after Palestinian terrorists had repeatedly crossed into Israel from Lebanon, Israeli forces attacked and overran PLO bases in the southern part of Lebanon, pushing the terrorists away from the border.

The IDF withdrew after two months, allowing UN forces to enter, but those troops couldn't prevent terrorists from coming back to the region, with new, more dangerous arms. Israeli strikes and commando raids also failed to stem the growth of this PLO army inside Lebanon.

As the PLO forces in Lebanon grew stronger, the situation in the Galilee in northern Israel became intolerable. Frequent attacks forced thousands of residents to flee their homes or spend large amounts of time in bomb shelters. In response, on June 6, 1982, the IDF moved 80,000 troops into Lebanon to drive out the terrorists in "Operation Peace for Galilee."

The Lebanon War

The mission met success initially, leading Israeli officials to broaden their objective. They decided that Israel would fight to expel the PLO from Lebanon and convince the country's leaders to sign a peace treaty. An agreement was reached, but Syria forced Lebanon to renege on the deal. Syrian troops had occupied

Look Closer

Through the years, Palestinians in the refugee camps in Jordan had become increasingly militant and powerful. By the late 1960s, they controlled the camps, openly brandished weapons, and had a strong enough army to threaten King Hussein's regime. The situation was exacerbated in September 1970 when Palestinian terrorists hijacked four commercial airplanes and flew three to Jordan and one to Cairo. After taking the passengers off the planes to hold as hostages, the planes were blown up. The captives, which included a number of Americans, were eventually traded for terrorists held in European jails.

The incident escalated the tension between the Palestinian radicals and the king, and armed clashes soon began to break out between the king's troops and the PLO. On September 19, 1970, Syrian tanks crossed the Jordanian border to support the Palestinians. The Israelis were prepared to intervene to defend Hussein, but Jordan's troops rallied and repulsed the Syrians.

Jordanian forces then turned on the PLO, killing and wounding thousands of Palestinians and forcing the leadership, along with thousands of refugees, into Syria and Lebanon. The incident came to be known among Palestinians as Black September.

much of Lebanon since that country's civil war in the 1970s, and Syrian president Hafez al-Assad insisted that his claims to the Golan Heights must be resolved before he would allow the Lebanese to sign a treaty with Israel.

The Israeli public united to support the war initially, but as it dragged on and expanded to include a siege of the Lebanese capital of Beirut, it provoked international criticism, Israelis began to debate the wisdom of continuing to fight. In August 1982, Yasser Arafat and most of the PLO fighters were expelled from Beirut to Tunisia, but Lebanese Muslims, upset by the Israeli

Word Work

Hezbollah *Hezbollah* (Party of God) is an Iranian- and Syrian-backed Islamic fundamentalist organization based in predominantly Shiite areas of southern Lebanon. The group was formed in 1982 and provides social services to Shiite-dominated communities. It also engages in terrorist attacks against Israel. Hezbollah seeks to take over Lebanon and create an Iranian-style Islamic republic and to destroy Israel. It has now become the dominant political power in the country.

army's presence in their country, soon began to attack Israeli forces.

On September 16 through 17, 1982, Israeli troops allowed Lebanese Christian Phalangist militiamen to enter two Beirut-area refugee camps, Sabra and Shatila, to root out Palestinian terrorist cells believed to be located there. The Israelis knew that the two groups had been warring for years and might have suspected that the Phalangists would seek revenge for past Palestinian massacres of Christians and the murders of Lebanese president Bashir Gemayel and twenty-five of his followers in a bomb attack by Palestinians earlier that week. By the time Israeli soldiers ordered the Phalangists out of the camps, they found hundreds dead (estimates range from 460 to 800), including women and children.

News of the massacre provoked international condemnation of Israel. The Phalangists, who perpetrated the crime, were spared the brunt of the criticism.

Israelis were also horrified by what had occurred; three hundred thousand attended a demonstration to condemn the killings. In what Henry Kissinger called a great tribute to Israeli democracy, the government appointed a commission to investigate, and the Kahan Commission of Inquiry found that Israel was indirectly responsible for not anticipating the possibility of Phalangist violence. Following publication of the report, General Raful Eitan, Israel's chief of staff, was dismissed, and Israeli defense minister Ariel Sharon resigned but remained a minister without portfolio in the government (meaning he could still vote in cabinet decisions but held no other responsibilities).

Lebanon Withdrawal

In July 1983, Israeli troops slowly began moving to end the war. As demands for an end to the fighting grew louder, Begin resigned as prime minister on September 15, 1983. In 1984, a coalition government of representatives of both Labor and Likud took office, with their leaders rotating as prime minister. The coalition leaders decided to withdraw from Lebanon, leaving behind a token force to patrol a security zone in southern Lebanon along Israel's border.

Although they had hoped this measure would be for only a short time, Israel wound up keeping troops in this area until May 2000. By that time, a total of 1,216 Israeli soldiers had been killed in the Lebanon War and deployment, many in skirmishes with the growing terrorist group Hezbollah.

PALESTINIANS REVOLT

Before Israelis could recover from the trauma of the war in Lebanon, and while their soldiers were still deployed there, violence erupted in the West Bank and Gaza Strip. In early December 1987, rumors that four Palestinians killed in a traffic accident in the Gaza Strip had really been murdered by Israelis provoked rioting that quickly escalated and sparked a wave of unrest that engulfed the West Bank, Gaza Strip, and Jerusalem. The violence came to be known as the Intifada.

During the first four years of the uprising, more than thirty-six hundred Molotov cocktail attacks, one hundred hand-grenade attacks, and six hundred assaults with guns or explosives were reported by the IDF The violence was directed at soldiers and civilians alike. In this period, sixteen Israeli civilians and eleven soldiers were killed by Palestinians

Word Work

Shiites *Shiites* make up the second-largest Muslim sect behind the Sunnis. The divide between Sunni and Shiite Muslims stems from the early days of Islam and arguments over Muhammad's successors. Iran, a non-Arab country, is the only Middle East nation with an overwhelming Shiite majority, but Iraq, Lebanon, and Bahrain have large Shiite communities.

Word Work

Intifada *Intifada* literally means "shaking off" and metaphorically "uprising" in Arabic. The term became associated with two periods of violent Palestinian protests and terror attacks, one beginning in December 1987, the other in September 2000.

in the territories, and more than fourteen hundred Israeli civilians and seventeen hundred Israeli soldiers were injured. Approximately eleven hundred Palestinians were killed in clashes with Israeli troops.

The PLO played a lead role in orchestrating the insurrection, although its leadership of the uprising was challenged by the fundamentalist Islamic organization Hamas, a violent group that rejects any peace negotiations with Israel.

The violence of the Intifada finally began to wane as the United States commenced its first showdown with Saddam Hussein after Iraq invaded Kuwait in 1990. The Palestinians had attracted international sympathy due to the perception that they were now the Davids fighting against an Israeli Goliath. When the PLO sided with Saddam, however, much of that support dissipated. In addition, the number of Arabs killed for political and other reasons by their fellow Palestinians began to exceed the number killed in clashes with Israeli troops.

Look Closer

In 1981, Israeli leaders became convinced Iraq was trying to produce a nuclear weapon and feared that Saddam Hussein would use it against them. To ensure this wouldn't happen, Menachem Begin ordered a daring surprise attack that destroyed the Osirak nuclear reactor. At the time, the attack was very controversial and roundly condemned. Years later, the move was praised for preventing Saddam Hussein from gaining nuclear weapons.

Word Work

Hamas *Hamas* is an Arabic acronym for the Islamic Resistance Movement, a fundamentalist Palestinian group that rejects all discussion of peace with Israel. Hamas has been responsible for many terrorist attacks against Israeli civilians and Palestinian collaborators with Israel. Hamas states in its charter that "The Day of Judgment will not come about until Muslims fight the Jews, when the Jew will hide behind stones and trees."

International attention shifted away from the Palestinian issue after the US-led coalition attacked Iraq in January 1991. During the war, Hussein fired thirty-nine missiles at Israel, killing four people and causing millions of dollars in damage. At the request of the United States, Israel decided not to retaliate, and the coalition quickly subdued Hussein's forces and liberated Kuwait.

The war with Iraq had nothing to do with Israel. The conflict between Israel and its neighbors was viewed as another cause of instability in the region, however, so US diplomats renewed efforts to negotiate a comprehensive peace.

CHAPTER TEN

WAGING PEACE

After the 1991 Gulf War, in which a US-led coalition forced Iraq to withdraw from Kuwait, American diplomats turned their attention again to the issues between Israel and the Palestinians. Because they recognized that an Israeli-Palestinian agreement was not likely until Arab states took steps toward peace with Israel, the Bush administration arranged a peace conference in 1991. Representatives of Syria, Lebanon, Jordan, and the Palestinians attended the conference in Madrid, which was cosponsored by the United States and the Soviet Union.

At the October 30 opening session, Israeli prime minister Yitzhak Shamir directly appealed to the Arab states to "speak in the language of reconciliation, coexistence, and peace with Israel." Arab representatives responded by harshly denouncing the Jewish state. Although the Madrid conference ended without

Have You Heard of Yitzhak Rabin? (1922-1995)

Yitzhak Rabin was the first Israeli prime minister who had been born in pre-state Israel. Born in Jerusalem in 1922, he became active in the Jewish paramilitary forces and in the War of Independence was an officer in the Palmach, an elite strike force within the Haganah. In 1953, Rabin was promoted to general.

As chief of staff of the IDF, a post he held from 1964 to 1968, he oversaw Israel's stunning victory in the Six-Day War. His foray into politics began as ambassador to the United States in 1968. Rabin was chosen to succeed Golda Meir as prime minister because of his record in the Six-Day War and his lack of connection to the government's ill-fated decisions leading up to the 1973 Yom Kippur War.

He resigned as prime minister in 1977 because of a financial scandal but was elected to the post again in 1992. During this term, he began the negotiations with the Palestinians that led to his receiving the Nobel Peace Prize in 1994, along with Shimon Peres and Yasser Arafat. He also signed a peace agreement between Israel and Jordan.

On November 4, 1995, Rabin was assassinated by a young, religious, Israeli Jew who believed the prime minister's policies were endangering the country and violated Jewish law.

any agreements, all the parties said they wanted to continue negotiations, and a series of talks was established. However, before more progress was made toward a concrete peace agreement, elections in the United States and Israel brought major changes in the policies of both governments.

When Bush was defeated in 1992, the Palestinians were forced to adjust to the new US president, Bill Clinton, who many people believed was far more sympathetic to Israel than Bush had been. At the same time, Yitzhak Rabin, who had again become prime minister, was considered more flexible than his predecessor. Rabin immediately showed he was willing to work with the Palestinians when he announced that no new Jewish settlements would be built in the Palestinian territories. As all sides adjusted to the new leadership in the early months of 1993, Israeli and Palestinian negotiators secretly tried to hammer out a compromise bearing some resemblance to what Begin had offered at Camp David.

SECRETS IN OSLO

Meanwhile, the Israelis were secretly negotiating directly with the PLO for the first time in Oslo, Norway. These negotiations were momentous, as Israeli government officials had never before talked directly with PLO members, refusing to negotiate because the organization's charter called for the destruction of Israel and because the PLO had been involved in so many acts of terrorism against Israelis.

A breakthrough in the relationship between Israel and Palestinians occurred when Israel agreed to recognize the PLO as the representative of the Palestinian

STRAIGHT from the Source

"We who have fought against you the Palestinians, we say to you today in a loud and clear voice, enough of blood and tears, enough."

—Yitzhak Rabin at White House ceremony, September 13, 1993

people. In exchange, PLO chairman Yasser Arafat agreed to recognize Israel, renounce terrorism, and revoke the provisions of the PLO charter that called for the destruction of the Jewish state. The formal Declaration of Principles (DOP) was signed on the White House lawn on September 13, 1993.

The DOP and subsequent agreements were referred to as the Oslo Accords and envisioned a five-year process to negotiate an end to the conflict between Israelis and Palestinians.. As part of the process, Israel agreed to give the Palestinians self-rule first in the Gaza Strip and Jericho, a town in the West Bank. The idea was to give the Palestinians authority over part of the disputed territories to help build confidence on both sides. If the arrangement worked, the Palestinians would see that Israel was sincerely willing to withdraw from the West Bank and Gaza Strip, and the Israelis would have a chance to judge if the Palestinians would pose a security threat if they turned over more land.

Later, the two sides were to negotiate the details of Palestinian autonomy for the rest of the territories. However, even before this process was completed, Israel agreed to give the Palestinians responsibility for health, education, welfare, taxation, tourism, and other civil functions throughout the West Bank. Israel kept responsibility for security throughout the disputed territories. The agreement called for the IDF to move out of heavily populated areas but not fully withdraw

Faces of Israel

Kiram, seventeen, was born in a village in the Galilee in northern Israel. She has a twin sister and an older brother. Her family owns a large agricultural farm, where they grow mainly olive trees. Her uncle used to be a member of the Knesset.

Kiram is Catholic and attends an all-girls school in Nazareth. She loves hiking in the Galilee forest and is working hard to improve both her Hebrew and English since she is a native Arabic speaker. She and her sister plan to attend university in Jerusalem.

from the territories, and all Israeli residents were allowed to remain in the West Bank and Gaza under Israel's protection.

Meanwhile, negotiators agreed to put off deciding the thorniest issues—the final borders separating Israelis and Palestinians, what to do about Palestinian refugees and Jewish settlements, and how to resolve both sides' demand that Jerusalem serve as their capital.

As the Israelis and Palestinians began to put their agreements into practice, Israel hoped momentum would be created for talks with its other neighbors.

Think about It

Why did the United States push for negotiations between Israel and the Palestinians?

???

JORDAN MAKES PEACE

In practical terms, Israel and Jordan had been at peace since 1967 and had quietly undertaken many cooperative activities. The Israelis had always believed it would be possible to reach an agreement with Jordan and viewed King Hussein as a reliable partner. But the king had never felt secure enough to formally declare peace with Israel because he was afraid of angering the Palestinians, his Arab neighbors, and his own people—more than half of whom were Palestinians.

However, when Israel and the Palestinians reached their own agreement, Hussein quickly entered formal negotiations, and, on October 26, 1994, Jordan became the second Arab country to sign a peace treaty with Israel.

Although no other Arab states were ready to sign formal treaties with Israel, several began allowing business and diplomatic contacts. By the end of 1994, more than 150 nations had diplomatic relations with Israel—more than double the number only a decade earlier.

SYRIA HOLDS OUT

For decades, Syrian president Hafez al-Assad had been the leader most responsible for blocking Arab nations from reaching peace agreements with Israel. He succeeded in keeping a united Arab front by demanding "justice for all or justice

STRAIGHT from the **Source**

"We are going to a war that has no dead or injured, no blood or suffering—the war for peace."

— YITZHAK RABIN QUOTE INSCRIBED ON THE WALL OF THE ISRAELI MINISTRY OF DEFENSE

for none," meaning that if Assad didn't get what he wanted, he would try to prevent any other Arab leader from reaching an agreement with Israel. But when Arafat and King Hussein of Jordan went ahead and made deals without his assent, Assad began to negotiate more seriously with Israel.

Assad insisted that Israel agree to a complete withdrawal from the Golan Heights before he would reveal what concessions he would make. Rabin hinted at a willingness to give up most of the Golan but only if Syria explained what sort of peace Israel could expect, making clear that he wanted relations similar to that between Israel and Egypt.

Because of Syria's tremendous influence over the Lebanese government, the stalemate with Syria also hindered progress in talks between Israel and Lebanon. Syria refused to allow Lebanon to negotiate with Israel before an agreement was reached regarding the Golan Heights. And Israel wanted Syria to sever its ties to Iran and stop supporting Hezbollah's objective of destroying Israel.

Israel and Syria negotiated off and on during the last half of the 1990s, but the two sides could never agree to a deal before Assad's death in 2000. Assad was succeeded by his son Bashar. The younger Assad gave no indication he would change his father's policies; he moved closer to Iran and intensified support for terrorist groups such as Hamas and Hezbollah. These developments made Israel even more suspicious of Syrian intentions and more reluctant to make territorial compromises. The result has been a continued Israeli-Syrian stalemate.

A PALESTINIAN STATE?

Prior to the Oslo Accords, Israel officially opposed the establishment of a Palestinian state because it believed such a state would pose a mortal danger to Israel's existence. The concern of Israeli officials was that the PLO might seek to carry out its "phased plan," which calls for the creation of a state in the territories that can then be used as a base to fight for control of the rest of Palestine, which would mean the destruction of the nation of Israel.

At that time, Israelis also worried about an increase in terrorism, the possibility of Islamic radicals wresting diplomatic control from Yasser Arafat, and the potential for a coalition of Arab forces to ally with the Palestinians in a future war. Moreover, if Israel were to withdraw to its pre-1967 borders, most of its population and industry would be within thirteen miles of hostile forces, and easily within range of the type of rockets Hamas fired from Gaza into southern Israel.

Despite the risks, more and more people in Israel gradually began to understand that mutually beneficial negotiations with the Palestinians could promote peace. Many supported the idea of establishing a Palestinian state in most of the West Bank and the entire Gaza Strip, believing that Israel could coexist with such a state—if the Palestinians were willing to live in peace.

Oslo II

Progress toward creating a Palestinian state was hampered by an unrelenting terrorist campaign, which took an ominous turn with a suicide bombing in January 1995. Still, Israelis and the Palestinians were able to sign a new agreement, which came to be known as Oslo II, at the White

Look Closer

Americans, who live in a country that stretches from the Atlantic to the Pacific, sometimes find it difficult to appreciate how geography affects the Arab-Israeli conflict. If forces hostile to Israel seized control of the West Bank, they could easily split Israel in two. At its narrowest point, the width of Israel prior to the Six-Day War was only nine miles, meaning a car traveling at sixty miles an hour could cross the whole country in nine minutes.

House on September 28, 1995. This agreement expanded the area of Palestinian self-rule beyond Gaza and Jericho into Bethlehem, Hebron, and Ramallah.

Israel agreed to withdraw its troops from six major West Bank cities and to dissolve the Israeli Civil Administration that had governed the territories, handing over governing responsibility to an elected Palestinian Council.

The Palestinian Authority, the new Palestinian administration led by Arafat, was now to be, at least nominally, in charge of territory that was divided into three areas:

- *Area A, which included six major West Bank cities.* The Palestinian Council was given complete responsibility for the civil administration and internal security there.
- *Area B, which included towns in other parts of the West Bank in which roughly 70 percent of the Palestinians lived.* The Council was given civil authority, but Israel kept overall security responsibility for safeguarding its citizens and preventing terrorism.
- *Area C, which covered the Jewish settlements, unpopulated areas, and regions deemed strategically important.* Israel retained full responsibility for security, but the Palestinian Council was given civil authority over health, education, and economics.

Look Closer

While Muslim tradition opposes suicide and the killing of innocent people, some radical Muslims believe they will be rewarded in the afterlife if they attack nonbelievers—people they consider infidels—or contribute to the liberation of Islamic territory. Many Palestinians have glorified people who carry out terrorist acts against Israelis, referring to the terrorists as martyrs. This is reflected in everything from the distribution of trading cards with pictures of "martyrs," to naming streets after terrorists, to Palestinian Authority-run television shows extolling the virtues of martyrdom.

Israel agreed to reduce troop levels at six-month intervals and free roughly two thousand Palestinian prisoners from its jails. For their part, the Palestinians agreed to revoke their charter articles calling for Israel's destruction within two months of the inauguration of the Palestinian Council.

Israelis Cautious

While most Israelis welcomed the chance for peace with the Palestinians, they believed Arafat's unwillingness or inability to prevent Arab terrorism created a huge obstacle to achieving that peace. Arafat was ruthless in dealing with his political opponents, having them jailed or murdered, but he would not act so decisively against members of the Palestinian Islamic Jihad and Hamas, two groups of Muslim extremists who vowed to destroy Israel.

Arafat had signed peace treaties with Israel, yet terrorism remained a tool he could and did use to accomplish his political objectives. He often used inflammatory rhetoric, speaking, for example, of liberating Jerusalem or declaring a jihad. Arafat's language assured Palestinians he had not lost his revolutionary zeal, and it frightened Israelis, who were also alarmed by venomous attacks made against them in the Palestinian media and in school textbooks used to teach young Palestinians in the West Bank and Gaza.

Although Israel continued to negotiate with Arafat, increasing numbers of Israelis were asking whether the peace process made sense. After all, if Arafat could not control the terrorists, what good was it to sign an agree-

Think about It

Why did Israel agree to withdraw from parts of the disputed territories?

? ? ?

Word Work

Jihad *Jihad* is derived from the Arabic verb *jahada*, which means "to exert." The word can apply to personal spiritual struggle; however, it is commonly rendered as "holy war." The word *jihad* has become associated with violence, because Islamic terrorists have claimed their actions are part of a jihad against Israel and the West.

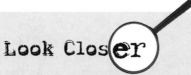

Look Closer

The PLO charter spelling out its objective of liberating Palestine was written in 1964. The charter was revised several times, but its language always made clear that the PLO's goal was to destroy Israel. As part of the Oslo Accords, the Palestinians agreed to revise the charter to remove this language. Though some have argued the PLO never followed the required procedure to do so, President Clinton certified that those clauses were annulled in 1998. The Hamas charter, meanwhile, continues to call for Israel's destruction.

ment with him? And if he could control them, he was obviously choosing not to and therefore was not really a partner for peace.

A STUNNING SETBACK

Even as some Israelis began to question the country's negotiations with the Palestinians, many others continued to approve of the efforts. On November 4, 1995, tens of thousands of Israelis assembled in downtown Tel Aviv to show their support for Israeli prime minister Rabin and the government's peace policies.

But as Rabin was leaving the rally, a religious Jew approached him from behind and shot him in the back. Rabin was rushed to the hospital, where he

STRAIGHT from the Source

"Legend has it that in every generation of Jews from time immemorial, a just leader emerged to protect his people and show them the way to safety. Prime Minister Rabin was such a leader."

—EULOGY FOR PRIME MINISTER RABIN BY PRESIDENT BILL CLINTON, NOVEMBER 6, 1995

What Would YOU Do?

You are a Palestinian living in the refugee camp in the city of Jenin in the West Bank. Your parents have told you stories about how your family lived in Jaffa and how the Jews forced them to leave during the war in 1948 that your teachers call Al-Nakba, "the Catastrophe." You have had little contact with Jews; the only ones you've seen are soldiers who guard checkpoints. On television, you see commentators call for liberating the homeland and programs suggesting that being a martyr for the cause of Palestine will allow you to enter paradise. At school, you study the history of Palestine, where you are taught that the Jews have no connection to the land. The maps in your textbooks show Palestine where you know Israel to be.

Many of your friends are involved in political organizations, and you know some who have been recruited to try to take bombs into Israel to blow up markets and buses.

You have several paths you can follow in your life, including joining a group that interacts with Israeli peace organizations or choosing to stay out of politics, focusing on your studies and trying to avoid trouble. But you could also join a group that advocates armed struggle that may ask you to try to attack Israelis.

What Really Happened

This episode in history hasn't closed. Young Palestinians face these types of choices every day.

Think About It

Why was Rabin's assassination especially painful for Israelis? What questions did it raise for Israeli society?

? ? ?

died shortly afterward. The killing shocked the nation. Most horrifying to most Israelis was the realization that Rabin had not been killed by a Palestinian or Arab opponent but by a Jew who believed the prime minister's policies had endangered the country. The murder was perhaps the most traumatic event in modern Israeli history—comparable to the impact on Americans of the assassination of John F. Kennedy. Rabin's killer, Yigal Amir, was arrested, tried, convicted of murder, and sentenced to life in prison.

Israel would continue its efforts to make peace with the Palestinians, but people all over the world realized that the loss of Rabin would have a major impact on future negotiations and actions.

CHAPTER ELEVEN

BALANCING PEACE AND SECURITY

As Israelis mourned Rabin and struggled to grasp the full impact of his assassination, his successor, Shimon Peres, began to consider the next major step in the peace process, which was supposed to be Israel's withdrawal of troops from most of the city of Hebron. However, a series of Palestinian terrorist attacks against Israel thwarted Peres's plan.

The escalation of violence also hurt Peres's popularity in Israel and led to a surge of support for the new Likud leader, Benjamin Netanyahu, who criticized the Oslo II agreement while insisting he could bring Israelis both peace and security. In May 1996, Netanyahu was narrowly elected prime minister.

After months of negotiations, on January 15, 1997, Netanyahu and Arafat reached a new agreement. The new deal specified that by August 31, 1998—the date when final status discussions (negotiations over the most difficult issues, including borders, settlements, refugees, and Jerusalem) would begin—Israel would move troops out of Hebron and end Israeli control in three more West Bank areas.

Netanyahu was obligated to follow through with the Hebron agreement, but continued terrorist attacks, inflammatory rhetoric by Arafat and other Palestinian officials, and opposition within his government caused him to postpone any further compromises.

TRYING TO MAKE A DEAL

The US government expressed displeasure at the Israeli government's hard-line approach to negotiations with the Palestinians and pressured Netanyahu to make more concessions. In response, at a meeting with Arafat and President Clinton in October 1998, Netanyahu agreed to withdraw Israeli forces from an additional 13 percent of the West Bank over a three-month period and to release 750 Palestinian prisoners.

In return, the Palestinians said they would arrest Palestinian terrorists, formally revoke the Palestinian charter's articles calling for Israel's destruction, and take measures to prevent the Palestinian media from stirring up hatred against Israel through articles and cartoons that were harshly critical of Israel and sometimes anti-Semitic—all steps they had promised to take in the original Oslo Accords but never did. Because this deal was made at the Wye River Plantation in Maryland, it became known as the Wye Agreement.

In December 1998, President Clinton made a historic trip to Gaza to witness the Palestine National Council (PNC) revise its charter to remove items that denied Israel's right to exist. Although some Israelis continued to insist that the procedure used by the Palestinians to revise the National Council's charter did

Have You Heard of Benjamin Netanyahu? (1949–)

Benjamin "Bibi" Netanyahu was born in Tel Aviv but spent his high school years in the United States, where his father taught history. After serving in the Israeli army, he received degrees in architecture and management from the Massachusetts Institute of Technology.

Returning to Israel in 1967, Netanyahu served in an elite anti-terror commando unit and took part in the rescue of hijacked Sabena Airlines hostages at Ben-Gurion Airport, during which he was wounded. In 1982, Netanyahu assumed the position of deputy chief of mission at the Israeli embassy in Washington and soon after was appointed Israel's ambassador to the United Nations. Netanyahu returned to Israel in 1988 and was elected to the Knesset as a Likud member and appointed deputy foreign minister.

Netanyahu was elected prime minister in 1996 but was defeated for reelection in 1999 by Ehud Barak. In early 2009, Netanyahu again became prime minister when he was asked to form a coalition government after closely divided elections in Israel.

not conform to the PLO's rules for amending the document, Netanyahu accepted the effort and moved to fulfill Israel's side of the agreement by carrying out the first phase of the promised withdrawal, surrendering control in what amounted to about 9 percent of the West Bank and releasing the required number of prisoners.

But the Palestinians did not live up to their side of the deal. They did not take necessary measures to prevent violence, arrest terrorists, confiscate

Have You Heard of Ehud Barak? (1942-)

Ehud Barak was born on Kibbutz Mishmar Hasharon. He joined the Israel Defense Forces in 1959 and served as a soldier and commander of an elite unit, and in various other command positions including tank brigade commander, armored division commander, and head of the IDF Intelligence Corps.

Barak is the most decorated soldier in Israeli history, having been awarded the Distinguished Service Medal and four other citations for courage and operational excellence. In April 1991, he became chief of the general staff and was promoted to the rank of lieutenant general, the highest rank in the military.

Following the agreement to grant Palestinians self-rule in the Gaza Strip and Jericho, Barak oversaw the redeployment of IDF troops in those areas, and he played a central role in finalizing the peace treaty with Jordan. He served as minister of foreign affairs from November 1995 until June 1996 and then as chairman of the Labor Party and a member of Knesset.

In May 1999, Barak defeated incumbent prime minister Benjamin Netanyahu and served as prime minister for two years. He was defeated in elections in 2001 and left politics for a while. He returned to head the Labor Party in 2007 and became the country's defense minister. In 2011, Barak formed a breakaway party with other Labor Party legislators called Atzmaut (Independence).

weapons, or reduce the size of their police force to the extent agreed to in the Oslo Accords.

Members of Netanyahu's governing coalition were incensed by what they viewed as a surrender to Arafat, to terrorism, and to US pressure. Other Israeli leaders supported the Wye Agreement but were dissatisfied because Netanyahu was not able to keep the peace process moving toward a final resolution of all outstanding issues. Because he had lost so much support, Netanyahu's government collapsed on December 21, 1998, and new elections were scheduled for May 1999.

New Israeli Leader, New Approach

Netanyahu's successor, Ehud Barak, promised to revitalize negotiations with both the Palestinians and the Syrians and to withdraw troops from Lebanon within a year—and to keep Israel safe during the process. He won over the electorate and defeated Netanyahu in a landslide.

Barak continued to cede to the Palestinians control of more areas of the territories, as had been agreed upon, and pledged to complete the process if the Palestinians complied with their obligations. Terrorist attacks against Israelis were increasing, however, suggesting that the Palestinians were not living up to their commitments to rein in terrorists or prevent violence against Israel.

Faces of Israel

Liora, seventeen, was born in Haifa, Israel's third-largest city. She is the youngest of three children in a family that has its roots in India and Eastern Europe. Liora is a secular Jew; she eats nonkosher food and rarely goes to synagogue. From an early age, she was involved in the Scouts organization, *Tzofim*, and recently became a group leader.

Liora enjoys outdoor activities, especially those at her city's beautiful beaches along the Mediterranean Sea. She also likes Israeli folk dancing and American pop music. One of her favorite experiences was working as a counselor at an American summer camp through the Scouts organization. After she finishes her mandatory two-year military service, Liora hopes to attend university and study law.

Arafat Turns Down Statehood

Barak decided that instead of prolonging the negotiating process, he would try to achieve a peace agreement that resolved all issues once and for all. President Clinton agreed to this idea and hosted a summit meeting with Arafat and Barak at Camp David in July 2000.

Barak laid out some dramatic new proposals that would have resulted in independence for the Palestinians, but Arafat rejected all US and Israeli ideas, while refusing to offer any of his own. In his proposal at Camp David, Barak became the first Israeli prime minister to agree to divide Jerusalem with the Palestinians, giving them sovereignty over Arab neighborhoods while retaining Israeli control over Jewish neighborhoods.

Barak's proposal included an offer that agreed to give approximately 97 percent of the West Bank and all of Gaza to the Palestinians. Also, Barak's plan apparently included an understanding that there would be an exchange of a small amount of pre-1967 Israeli territory for areas where large Jewish settlements were located close to the Green Line. Most settlements were to be dismantled. But the parties did not reach an agreement on the Palestinian refugee issue, and Arafat dismissed the compromises Barak offered.

Look Closer

In a conversation three days before President Clinton's term ended, Yasser Arafat told Clinton that he was a great man. The president responded, "The hell I am. I'm a colossal failure, and you made me one."

Clinton Parameters

Still, Barak did not give up trying to negotiate a peace agreement, and Palestinian and Israeli teams met again at the White House in December 2000. Eventually, President Clinton offered a series of compromise proposals, now called the Clinton Parameters, which involved even more Israeli concessions than Barak had offered at Camp David. The parameters would have allowed Palestinians to establish the Arab neighborhoods of East Jerusalem as their capital and granted them sovereignty over the Temple Mount; Israel's capital city would have covered the remainder

Have You Heard of Ariel Sharon? (1928–)

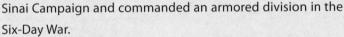

Sharon was born in Israel on February 27, 1928, and earned a law degree from the Hebrew University of Jerusalem. During the 1948 War of Independence, he commanded an infantry company. In 1953, he founded and led a special commando unit that carried out retaliatory operations against Palestinian terrorists; he later fought in the Sinai Campaign and commanded an armored division in the Six-Day War.

Sharon resigned from the army that year but was recalled during the 1973 Yom Kippur War to again command an armored division, leading the crossing of the Suez Canal that helped secure an Israeli victory.

Sharon was elected to the Knesset in 1973 but resigned a year later, serving as security adviser to Prime Minister Yitzhak Rabin. In 1981, Sharon was appointed defense minister, serving in this post during the Lebanon War. In 1983, Sharon resigned after a government commission found him indirectly responsible for the 1982 massacre of Palestinians at the Sabra and Shatila refugee camps that had been carried out by Lebanese militias.

Sharon returned to government, serving in a variety of cabinet positions. He was appointed foreign minister in 1998 and elected prime minister in 2001. Sharon's decision to evacuate Jews living in the Gaza Strip in 2005 caused a split in his Likud party, leading him to form a new centrist party—Kadima.

On January 4, 2006, Sharon suffered a serious stroke, which left him comatose. He was succeeded as prime minister by Ehud Olmert.

Think about It

What strategies might Israel use to balance security concerns with the rights of the Palestinians?

???

of Jerusalem, and Israel would have controlled the area beneath the Temple Mount, including the Western Wall.

Barak accepted the parameters, but many Israelis believed he offered the Palestinians too much, especially the division of Jerusalem. Some members of the Palestinian delegation were inclined to accept the offer even though it fell short of their demands. The final decision rested with Arafat, however, who rejected the deal without making a counteroffer. The reason for Arafat's rejection of the settlement, according to Dennis Ross, America's chief Middle East peace negotiator, was the clause specifying that the agreement meant the end of the conflict. "For him to end the conflict is to end himself," said Ross. Daniel Kurtzer, former US ambassador to Israel and Egypt concurred: "The failure of Camp David is largely attributed to the fact that Arafat did not even negotiate....It didn't matter what he put on the table; he put nothing on the table."

SECOND INTIFADA

On September 28, 2000, a few months after Barak met with Arafat at Camp David, Israeli leader Ariel Sharon made a controversial visit to the Temple Mount in Jerusalem. At the time, Sharon was the leader of the Likud Party, the party that stood in opposition to Barak's Labor Party, and a controversial figure to Palestinians who blamed him for violence that occurred in Lebanese refugee camps in 1982.

The next day, a large number of Palestinians demonstrated at the site, and violence erupted between them and Israeli police. In the following days this event mushroomed into what is called the Second Intifada, popularly referred to by the Palestinians as the "Al-Aqsa Intifada."

Palestinians blamed Sharon's trip for the outbreak of violence, but the violence had actually been planned by Arafat much earlier. The Second Intifada gradually escalated; Palestinian terror attacks and Israeli counterattacks continued for nearly five years, claiming the lives of more than one thousand Israelis and three thousand Palestinians.

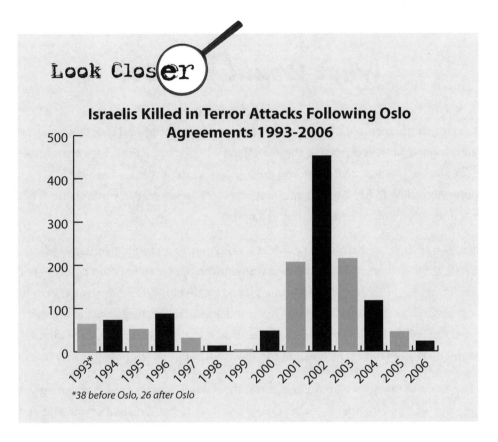

Look Closer

Israelis Killed in Terror Attacks Following Oslo Agreements 1993-2006

*38 before Oslo, 26 after Oslo

Sharon Comes to Power

By December 2000, the Second Intifada was in full force, and many Israelis were upset that Barak's policy of compromise was being met by a renewal of Palestinian violence. Sharon, running against Barak for the position of prime minister, criticized the concessions Barak had proposed, especially the idea of dividing Jerusalem, and argued that he was the one who could bring Israel peace and security. Israeli voters agreed with Sharon, electing him by a landslide in February 2001.

Almost immediately after Sharon took office, a series of horrific suicide bombings tested his promise to provide security to his people. Sharon sent the army into the territories for counterstrikes, but they seemed to have little effect.

International pressure began to build on Sharon to resume negotiations, with many world leaders saying the Palestinians needed some hope of achieving their political goals to prevent them from turning to violence. But Sharon main-

What Would YOU Do?

Israeli teenagers serving in the army are often forced to make difficult life-and-death decisions in a matter of moments. Imagine you are in the Israeli army and face this situation: You are assigned to a checkpoint in the West Bank where many Palestinians cross into Israel for work or medical treatment. You must search each person and vehicle for weapons. According to intelligence information you have received, an ambulance is expected to arrive with a terrorist carrying a bomb.

Suddenly an ambulance arrives, and inside is a woman who is seemingly pregnant. You know that at other checkpoints in the past women who appeared to be pregnant were not, and in fact were actually carrying equipment for a suicide bomb. But the woman in front of you appears to be in pain, and the man with her claims to be her husband and appears very anxious. The ambulance driver says the woman is about to give birth, and without the proper medical attention at the hospital, the newborn baby will struggle to survive.

It's a hot day, and many cars are waiting at the checkpoint. A news crew is watching your actions, and your commander is yelling on the two-way radio: "Don't let ambulances go through because there's a terrorist in an ambulance!"

You have to make a decision. If you let the ambulance go through and it contains a terrorist with a bomb, then innocent people may die. But if there isn't a terrorist in the ambulance and the woman is exactly what she appears to be, you may cause her to lose her child.

What would you do?

What Really Happened

The soldier called for an ambulance to come to the checkpoint from the Israeli side of the border. The woman and her husband were then allowed to get into that ambulance and continue to the hospital, while the other vehicle was kept at the border until it could be searched more thoroughly.

Look Closer

The Israeli government faces the nearly impossible task of protecting its civilian population from terrorists who are prepared to blow themselves up. One strategy Israel has used to stop the terrorists is to find and kill them before they can do harm.

Targeting the terrorists in this way has a number of advantages. First, it places a price on terror, letting would-be terrorists know that Israelis cannot be attacked with impunity and that if they target others, they should be prepared to become targets themselves. Second, it preempts terror strikes, eliminating those who would harm Israelis. Third, it disrupts terrorists' plans, forcing them to stay on the move, revise strategies, and work much harder to carry out their goals.

The policy also has costs. Israel is frequently condemned by other nations for its actions, which some believe risk killing innocent people. Israel also risks revealing the identity of informers, who often provide the information needed to find the terrorists, and puts its soldiers in danger as they carry out what are sometimes high-risk operations. And opponents of these targeted killings argue that they do no good because they perpetuate a cycle of violence: Every time the Israelis attack, the terrorists seek revenge.

tained that the violence had to stop first and said negotiating "under fire" would send the message that Israel could be forced by terror to make concessions.

More Terror

The violence grew worse as more and more Palestinians strapped explosives to their bodies and blew themselves up along with Israeli men, women, and children. And in September 2001, terrorists murdered Israeli tourism minister Rehavam Ze'evi.

STRAIGHT from the Source

"It is untenable for Israeli citizens to live in terror. It is untenable for Palestinians to live in squalor and occupation. And the current situation offers no prospect that life will improve. Israeli citizens will continue to be victimized by terrorists, and so Israel will continue to defend herself, and the situation of the Palestinian people will grow more and more miserable. My vision is two states, living side by side, in peace and security. There is simply no way to achieve that peace until all parties fight terror."

—PRESIDENT GEORGE W. BUSH, JUNE 24, 2002

In January 2002, Israeli forces stopped the *Karine A*, a Palestinian freighter on its way to the Suez Canal. The ship was carrying fifty tons of weapons from Iran that were paid for by one of Arafat's top aides. Arafat told President George W. Bush he did not know about the ship, but its capture proved that Arafat remained involved in terrorism. This convinced Bush that Sharon was correct; Arafat could not be trusted.

Bush Offers Plan

On June 24, 2002, President Bush laid out a plan that called on the Palestinians to "change Palestinian leadership," reform the governmental institutions of the Palestinian Authority, adopt democratic and free-market principles, and end terrorism. He called on other Arab nations to cease their support of terrorism and normalize relations with Israel, and urged Syria to close its terrorist camps and expel terrorist organizations.

Israel was not required to do anything until the violence ceased, but later Bush began pressing Israel to withdraw troops from the West Bank and Gaza and negotiate a final settlement that would include a withdrawal to secure and defensible borders. The president said that if the Palestinians fulfilled their obligations, he would support the creation of a "provisional" state of Palestine after

What Would YOU Do?

You are the chief of staff for the IDF. You have just received word from secret sources that the leader of the terrorist group Hamas and all of his top lieutenants soon will be meeting in an apartment building in downtown Gaza City. The air force has told you that a two-thousand-pound bomb would destroy the building in which they are meeting but would probably damage surrounding buildings and kill some innocent Palestinians as well.

You could ignore the meeting because it is being held in a highly populated area. Or you could order a ground assault, but that would involve sending troops into the heart of enemy territory.

What Really Happened

The IDF decided to bomb the building but with a much smaller bomb. Because of that, the building was only slightly damaged and all the terrorists escaped. However, no innocent people were injured.

three years, with the expectation that the state's final borders and complete sovereignty would be resolved in negotiations with Israel.

The Palestinians did not seem to seriously respond to Bush's plan. Although they did take some steps to institute reforms, the violence against Israel continued. Bombings of shopping malls, restaurants, discos, and buses became all too common. The terrorists were proving nearly impossible to stop because they were prepared to die and because they knew that after their deaths, they would be considered martyrs, heroes who had died to end Israeli occupation. Families of suicide bombers were given money by the Palestinian Authority (some of which came from Saudi Arabia and Iraq) to compensate them for their losses.

The Security Fence

Most of the suicide attacks were not directed at soldiers but at civilians. After more than eight hundred Israelis were killed in terrorist incidents, the Israeli government decided in 2002 to build a security fence to make it more difficult for terrorists to infiltrate the country from the West Bank.

Israelis had resisted building a fence for thirty-five years, but the violence had reached such a level that a decision was made to build the type of barrier that already existed on Israel's borders with Lebanon, Jordan, and Syria. Most of the barrier is a fence and not a wall, but a few miles are made of concrete in places where it is necessary to prevent Palestinian snipers from shooting at Israeli motorists.

Although the fence has proved successful in preventing attacks, it is also controversial because it was built in part on areas claimed or owned by Palestinians. The United Nations and the International Court of Justice condemned Israel for building the fence, and even some Israelis have criticized the route of the barrier because it was not built exactly along the Green Line that had effectively defined the border between Israel and Jordan before 1967.

Deciding the Route

From a strategic point of view it made little sense to build the fence along the Green Line, because that border would not have been the best place to prevent terrorist infiltrations. Israeli leaders also decided not to build the fence along this line because large numbers of Israelis would have been on the Palestinian side of the fence. Part of the route was designed to include major settlements that the government expected eventually to incorporate into Israel. This idea was controversial because Palestinians and many others believed Israel should dismantle *all* settlements, regardless of where they were.

Think about It

The United States uses drones to kill terrorists. This is similar to Israel's policy of the targeted killing of terrorists. What are the moral, legal, and military concerns associated with this policy? What would you advise a leader to do to stop terrorists?

But the settlements included within the fenced area are, essentially, large cities, and Israel has no intention of giving up those areas. By implication, Israeli leaders suggest that those settlements not included within the fence eventually will be evacuated, and the land will become part of a future Palestinian state.

Palestinians and their supporters who opposed the fence petitioned the Israeli Supreme Court to block its construction or change its route. The court ruled that Israel had a right to build a fence to protect its citizens but said it had to balance the need for security with the harm it did to people living along the route of the fence, ordering the government to alter the route in places and take account of the fence's impact on the Palestinians. The Israeli government complied with the Supreme Court's orders.

NEW ROAD MAP

While Israel built the fence in hopes of improving its security, the international community hoped to stop the violence and rejuvenate the peace process by building on the proposals made by President Bush. On April 30, 2003, Bush—on behalf of the "Quartet," made up of the United States, European Union, Russia, and the United Nations—announced a new "road map" for peace.

The proposal called for a two-state solution to the Israeli-Palestinian conflict and laid out a series of steps each side should take toward that goal, starting with the Palestinian leadership acting decisively against terror and Israel taking actions that would include freezing all settlement activity. The Quartet laid out a timetable for the Palestinians to stop the violence and enact a variety of reforms while Israel pursued its required steps.

The world leaders wanted to establish a Palestinian state living in peace beside Israel by the end of 2005, but it quickly became clear that the timetable was unrealistic. Palestinian leadership failed to stop the violence, and Israel declared it had no obligation to end settlement activity until the terror ceased. The Palestinians said they would not stop their attacks until Israel left the territories.

As a result, violence increased, more Jews settled in the West Bank, and hope grew dim that the road map would succeed in the near future.

CHAPTER TWELVE

TESTING "LAND FOR PEACE"

I n late 2003, when it seemed that Israelis and Palestinians were at a stalemate in their efforts to end the conflict between them, Israel's prime
minister, Ariel Sharon, startled the world by proposing that Israel withdraw
all Israeli troops from the Gaza Strip and evacuate all the Jews living there
and in four settlements in a small area of the West Bank. Even more surprising, Sharon said he was ready to take these steps without demanding
any moves in return by the Palestinians.

The plan shocked many Israelis; Sharon was considered a hawk because he often advocated using military force to suppress Palestinian violence and because he was a vigorous advocate of building Jewish communities in the Palestinian territories. In addition, when Sharon was campaigning for reelection as prime minister earlier in 2003, he had criticized his opponent's plan to withdraw unilaterally from parts of the territories, the very move he was now making.

Sharon's position on Jewish settlements in the territories had evolved, however, as he became convinced that it made little sense to devote resources—in particular, Israeli soldiers—to defend eighty-five hundred Jews living among more than one million Palestinians. Furthermore, he believed Israel could never annex the Gaza Strip because the Palestinians living there would then become Israeli citizens, making it more difficult for Israel to remain a Jewish state. Sharon concluded that the prospect for peace and security for Israel would be enhanced by disengaging from Gaza. The Palestinians would also benefit by no longer being subject to Israeli authority, and they would have the chance to start to build their state.

Look Closer

The Gaza Strip comprises about 140 square miles, roughly twice the size of Washington, DC. After Israeli forces captured the area from Egypt in 1967, the government began to encourage Jews to move there in the early 1970s. The population slowly grew until a total of seventeen hundred families lived in twenty-one settlements in Gaza.

After the Oslo agreements, the Palestinian Authority assumed control over about 80 percent of the area. But escalating violence, especially after September 2000, led Israel to impose stricter restrictions on Palestinians in the area and to engage in frequent military operations to prevent terrorist attacks.

The decision to evacuate Gaza and four West Bank settlements caused great upheaval in Israel as Jewish settlers living in Gaza and their supporters protested the idea. Jews living elsewhere in the West Bank were especially vocal because they feared they might be asked to leave their homes next. Many Israelis also argued that it was unfair to ask Jews to move out of Gaza after the government had encouraged them to move there in the first place in the interests of creating a security foothold there.

Still, many Israelis supported Sharon's plan, and the Knesset in October 2004 voted to approve the plan, even though Sharon's

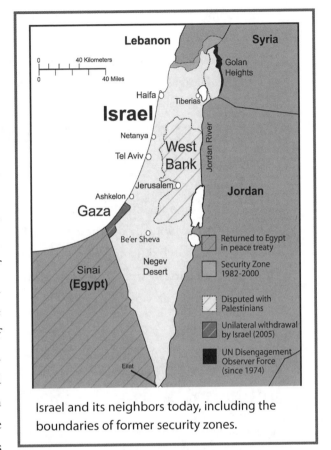

Israel and its neighbors today, including the boundaries of former security zones.

own party voted against it. Protests against the plan became so heated that some feared Israel might be on the verge of a civil war.

ARAFAT DIES

In the midst of the heated debates over Sharon's plan, Yasser Arafat suddenly died in November 2004, and many people around the world expressed the hope that his death would remove an obstacle to peace in the region. Arafat had been the unquestioned leader of the Palestinians for decades but was viewed by the Israeli government, and ultimately by the Bush administration and many world leaders, as an immovable obstacle to a peace agreement.

Arafat was replaced by Mahmoud Abbas, a man who had negotiated with Israel in the past and who was seen to be a potential partner for peace. It soon became apparent, however, that Abbas did not have the ability to stop the ongoing violence against Israel.

ISRAEL CLOSES SETTLEMENTS

Israel, meanwhile, went ahead with plans to close Jewish settlements in the Gaza Strip, offering Jews in Gaza money to resettle elsewhere. But many still refused to leave their homes. Finally, the army was sent to physically remove anyone who had not left voluntarily by August 17, 2005.

Though some skirmishes occurred during the evacuation process, the operation went relatively smoothly. Most of the settlers protested peacefully, and the soldiers sent to carry out the evacuation acted with great sensitivity to make the

Have You Heard of Mahmoud Abbas? (1935-)

Mahmoud Abbas, also known as Abu Mazen, was born in Safed on March 26, 1935. He left as a refugee for Syria in 1948 and worked as an elementary school teacher before earning a Ph.D. in history. He was a founding member of Fatah and a member of the Palestine National Council and the PLO Executive Committee.

He returned to the territories in September 1995 and in March 2003 was named the first prime minister of the Palestinian Authority. However, he never had full authority because Yasser Arafat insisted that all decisions be cleared with him. Abbas wound up resigning in frustration after just four months in office. Following Arafat's death, Abbas was elected president of the Palestinian Authority on January 9, 2005.

Faces of Israel

Oudi, seventeen, is part of the third generation of his family to live in the town of
Yerucham in the Negev desert. His grandparents came to Israel from
Morocco in the late 1950s. His father is a bus driver, and his mother serves
as a nurse in the regional hospital in the city of Be'er Sheva.

Oudi is a big fan of basketball and loves to watch Israeli, American, and
European professional teams on television. Oudi plays basketball for his
town's local team and enjoys traveling every two weeks to other areas in
Israel to play games. Besides sports, Oudi loves films and is hoping to learn
to become a filmmaker after his military service.

traumatic process of removing Jews from their homes as painless as possible.
Many thought the evacuation might take months to complete, but it was done
in only a few weeks.

As the Palestinians had requested, Israel destroyed all of the houses belonging to the settlers but left behind greenhouses built by Israeli farmers so the
Palestinians could use them to build their economy.

Gaza after the Withdrawal

Most Israelis hoped that when they ended thirty-eight years of military rule in
Gaza the Palestinians would respond by stopping violence against Israel and
taking steps to build the infrastructure for their own state. For years, peace
activists had said Israel should trade land for peace, and now here was a test case.
Israel had given up land; would the Palestinians offer peace in return? The
answer came quickly when Palestinian terrorists fired rockets from Gaza into
Israel and began building up their arsenal by smuggling weapons from Egypt.

Over the course of the next three years, terrorists in Gaza attacked Israel
with thousands of rockets and mortars, and the Palestinian Authority was

Palestinians sometimes claim they are descendants of the Canaanites and were in Israel before the Israelis. But there is no evidence they are related to the Canaanites, who disappeared three thousand years ago. In fact, no one knows if any of the Canaanites' descendants survived or what ethnic or national identity they would have if they had survived. The Palestinians can trace their origins to the seventh century, when people from Arabia swept into Palestine as they conquered lands in the Middle East. From that point until the early twentieth century, the Palestinian population was small and only began to grow significantly in the twentieth century, after Jewish immigrants began to improve the quality of health care and create economic opportunities that attracted Arabs from neighboring areas.

unable or unwilling to stop them. During this time, the Palestinians made little progress toward building a state and proved to be violent rather than peaceful neighbors, which made Israelis increasingly reluctant to make additional territorial concessions.

Hamas and Fatah

The situation worsened when Hamas won the Palestinian election in 2006. Since that election, Hamas and the rival Palestinian leadership from Abbas's Fatah movement have fought for power in the Palestinian Authority.

Hamas has a significant voice in the Palestinian government, refuses to recognize Israel or renounce terrorism, and says it will not honor past agreements that Arafat had signed with Israel. Consequently, Israel has refused to negotiate with Hamas, and the international community has imposed restrictions on financial aid to the Palestinian Authority for as long as Hamas refuses to recognize Israel's right to exist and renounce violence.

STRAIGHT from the Source

"Nobody does Israel any service by proclaiming its 'right to exist.' Israel's right to exist, like that of the United States, Saudi Arabia and 152 other states, is axiomatic and unreserved. Israel's legitimacy is not suspended in midair awaiting acknowledgment. There is certainly no other state, big or small, young or old, that would consider mere recognition of its 'right to exist' a favor, or a negotiable concession."

—ABBA EBAN, FORMER ISRAELI FOREIGN MINISTER IN THE *NEW YORK TIMES*, NOVEMBER 18, 1981

After about fifteen months of attempted coexistence and even a national unity government between Hamas and Fatah, Hamas seized power in Gaza in June 2007 in a violent coup. This action led Palestinian Authority leader Mahmoud Abbas to appoint a new caretaker government in the West Bank that was committed to ending Hamas's political rule. While Israeli leaders agreed to talk with Abbas, he did not represent all Palestinians, and most Israelis did not believe he had the ability to sign or implement any agreements.

THE SECOND LEBANON WAR

The failure of Israel's disengagement from Gaza to bring progress toward peace wasn't the only setback during this time. In 2000, Israel had also unilaterally withdrawn its troops from southern Lebanon, where they had been stationed since Israel invaded in 1982. Israeli leaders had hoped that when their troops left Lebanon, the Lebanese government would then deploy its army along the border to disarm terrorists and maintain order, but that did not happen. Instead, Iran and Syria supported Hezbollah attacks on soldiers and civilians in northern Israel while Hezbollah continued to build its terrorist network.

In July 2006, Hezbollah raiders crossed the border, killed three Israeli soldiers, and kidnapped two others. Ehud Olmert, who had taken over as prime minister after Sharon suffered a debilitating stroke in January of that year, ordered an attack on Hezbollah. Fighting escalated as Hezbollah began to fire thousands of rockets into northern Israel. Over the course of one month, more than four thousand rockets landed in Israel, and hundreds of thousands of Israelis were forced to evacuate their homes or live in bomb shelters.

Although Israel had been attacked first, the ferocity of its counterattacks on Hezbollah caused international opinion to turn against it. As Lebanese casualties began to mount, pressure grew on Israel to accept a ceasefire. In August, the United Nations adopted a resolution calling for Israeli troops to withdraw and

Have You Heard of Ehud Olmert? (1945-)

Ehud Olmert was born in Binyamina, Israel, in 1945. He served in the IDF as a combat infantry unit officer and was a military correspondent for the IDF journal *Bamachane*. A lawyer, he also holds degrees in psychology and philosophy. Olmert was elected to the Knesset in 1973 and served as a minister in the government from 1988 until 1992. In 1993, Olmert was elected mayor of Jerusalem. He resigned a decade later to return to the Knesset.

In 2003, Olmert was appointed minister of industry and trade, and deputy prime minister. Olmert became an influential member of the cabinet and was one of the first to advocate a withdrawal from Gaza, an idea that ultimately was endorsed by Prime Minister Ariel Sharon. In 2005, Olmert joined Sharon and several other former Likud ministers to form the new centrist party Kadima.

On January 4, 2006, Sharon suffered a massive stroke that left him unable to perform his duties as prime minister. Olmert became acting prime minister at that time and was elected prime minister on March 28, 2006, when Kadima received the most votes in the election to the Knesset. He left office in 2009.

for an international peacekeeping force to be deployed along the border to prevent Hezbollah from rearming and threatening Israel.

The Lebanese government was also required to disarm Hezbollah, yet doing so might have provoked a civil war in the country and it was unwilling to follow through. The Lebanese army did finally move into southern Lebanon, and the strengthened UN peacekeeping force helped to provide a modicum of needed stability on Israel's northern border.

Nevertheless, in Israel, the Second Lebanon War was widely viewed as a complete failure. Despite its superior firepower, Israeli forces failed to destroy Hezbollah as a fighting force, and the Israeli government had not been able to prevent its citizens from coming under a barrage of rockets. Later, Israelis learned that the Israeli Air Force had destroyed longer-range rockets that Hezbollah had planned to use against Israel's major cities, but questions were still raised about how the war was managed. Israelis were also shocked when they learned that the army was ill-prepared to fight a war of this kind and that many soldiers were sent into battle without the equipment they needed.

Israel's northern border remains a source of concern today, because Hezbollah, with Iranian backing, has essentially taken over Lebanon. Despite a UN resolution and force calling for Hezbollah to be disarmed and smuggling to be halted, Hezbollah has received a steady stream of aid and arms from Iran and Syria. Hezbollah now has tens of thousands of rockets pointed in Israel's direction.

OPERATION CAST LEAD

The Gaza Strip also continues to be a source of worry for Israelis. When Hamas took over Gaza, it began to bombard southern Israel with mortars and rockets, firing nearly ten thousand over a three-year period. Though only a few Israelis were killed in these attacks, many were injured, and much of the population lived in constant fear, with less than fifteen seconds to find shelter after an alarm sounded to indicate an incoming rocket. Sometimes there was no warning at all.

For three years, Israel launched only limited military operations against the terrorists. However, when Hamas started to fire more accurate and long-range

Faces of Israel

Samir, sixteen, is from Daliyat el-Carmel, in northwest Israel, where his entire family lives. Samir belongs to Israel's Druze minority. His family owns a traditional restaurant, which is very popular among tourists in the region.

In addition to attending school, Samir helps his family run the restaurant and loves to welcome strangers to their village. Proud to be an Israeli, Samir hopes to join a combat unit in the military and become an officer like his older brother.

rockets that reached deeper into Israel and put nearly one million civilians at risk, Prime Minister Olmert launched Operation Cast Lead, on December 27, 2008, sending troops into the Gaza Strip to stop the rocket fire.

The battle lasted only a few weeks, with Israel signing a ceasefire initiated by Egyptian president Hosni Mubarak on January 18, 2009, but approximately fourteen hundred Palestinians were killed during the fighting. Although more than half were believed to have been associated with Hamas, many innocent people died as well: in many cases the terrorists used them as shields and fired their rockets from civilian areas. Though the Israeli government and army took significant measures to avoid the loss of innocent lives—phoning homes, dropping leaflets warning people to leave, and firing warning shots—civilians sometimes were caught in the crossfire.

Although Israel agreed to the ceasefire and withdrew its troops from the Gaza Strip, its leaders made it clear that they would again use force if the rocket fire continued to threaten its population.

Israel successfully stopped the rocket barrages, though terrorists periodically fired mortars or rockets into southern Israel in the following years. Israel's ability to defend itself without mounting a large-scale military operation was greatly enhanced in 2011 when the Iron Dome antimissile defense system was

The alarm goes off, signaling that a rocket is inbound. Imagine trying to get your family to safety in less than fifteen seconds. What if you have elderly parents or a disabled child?

Nine-year-old Tzahar is a resident of Sderot. He's deaf and can't hear the alarm. As a result, he's been injured twice by rockets fired from the Gaza Strip.

Osher and Rami Twito, brothers ages eight and eighteen, were walking home through the town square when the warning siren rang out. They tried to take cover but didn't make it. A rocket landed nearby and sprayed them with shrapnel. Osher, who loved soccer, had a leg amputated that night and now must use a wheelchair. Rami had a lengthy operation to repair a severe break in his leg.

Their parents moved to Ashdod, a city they thought was beyond rocket range. Now, with technology obtained from Iran, Hamas has fired missiles from Gaza that hit Ashdod and beyond.

deployed. Iron Dome proved successful in intercepting some of the longer-range missiles that Hamas targeted at Israel's larger cities in the south. Other citizens, however, especially in Sderot, continued to rely on the alarm system that gives them only fifteen seconds from the time the siren sounds to find shelter.

HAMAS AND THE GOLDSTONE REPORT

Another outcome of Operation Cast Lead was widespread international criticism of Israel's use of force, which some people considered disproportionate. The UN Human Rights Council appointed a fact-finding commission to investigate whether any violations of international humanitarian law had taken place during the conflict between Israel and Hamas. Named after its chairman, South African jurist Richard Goldstone, the Goldstone Report, largely based on unverified accounts by Palestinians and non-governmental organizations, was highly critical of Israel's conduct. It also paid scant attention to the three years of Hamas rocket bombardment of Israeli towns and villages that led up to the operation. Investigators made little effort to probe Hamas activities before or during Operation Cast Lead and found no evidence that Hamas fired rockets from civilian homes; that terrorists hid among the civilian population, fired mortars, antitank missiles, and machine guns into Palestinian villages when IDF forces were in proximity; or that Hamas seized and booby-trapped Palestinian civilian houses to ambush IDF soldiers. The findings directly contradicted photos, video, and reports by journalists that showed and described Hamas militants participating in all of these illegal activities.

Even UN Humanitarian Affairs official John Holmes had criticized Hamas for "the reckless and cynical use of civilian installations . . . and indiscriminate firing of rockets against civilian populations," which he characterized as "clear violations of international law."

On April 1, 2011, Goldstone retracted his accusations that Israel had intentionally targeted civilians and was guilty of war crimes during its conflict with Hamas. He said Israel had the "right and obligation to defend itself and its citizens against such attacks." In fact, as Colonel Richard Kemp, former commander of British forces in Afghanistan, testified to the Goldstone committee in 2009, "The IDF did more to safeguard the rights of civilians in a combat zone than any other army in the history of warfare."

FLOTILLA FALLOUT

One of the other consequences of the violence in Gaza was that Israel imposed a blockade on the area to prevent the smuggling of weapons. The blockade was backed by Western nations that continued to insist that Hamas recognize Israel and end terrorism, and it was enforced on Gaza's southern border by Egypt. Once again Israel came under criticism for allegedly denying humanitarian goods to Palestinians in Gaza. The Israeli government, in fact, allowed food, medicine, and other items to be transported by humanitarian organizations but also insisted on being able to check shipments for contraband.

In the spring of 2010, a group of pro-Palestinian activists, part of a coalition called the Free Gaza Movement, decided to challenge the Israeli blockade by sailing ships full of supplies from Turkey directly to Gaza. Israeli officials agreed to accept the goods at one of its ports and transfer them to Gaza, but the flotilla organizers refused.

When six ships approached Israeli waters off the coast of Gaza on May 31, 2010, Israeli naval forces met them in international waters. When confronted, five of the six ships agreed to sail to Ashdod after being boarded by Israeli naval personnel. When Israeli naval personnel boarded the sixth ship, the *Mavi Marmara*, they were ambushed by passengers on deck wielding clubs, bats, pipes, and knives. The passengers wrestled one of the naval commandos to the ground, stripped him of his handgun, and threw him over the side, where he landed on a lower deck, thirty feet below, and suffered serious head trauma. At this point the commandos fired on passengers who attacked them, some of whom had handguns that they had taken from commandos. By the end of the fighting, nine passengers were dead and seven Israeli soldiers were wounded.

Though the Israelis were defending themselves, Israel was again criticized for its use of force. The Turkish government was especially angry, since its citizens were injured, and insisted on an apology. The Israeli government refused to apologize for its soldiers defending themselves, which precipitated a crisis in Turkish-Israel relations. The tension in the relationship is potentially serious for Israel's security and regional standing since Turkey has been one of its most important allies.

CAPTIVE SOLDIERS

Terrorists from Hamas and Hezbollah have kidnapped Israeli soldiers, with the goal of exchanging them for prisoners held in Israeli jails. On a number of occasions terrorists have forced Israel to make lopsided trades. In 1985, for

What Would YOU *Do?*

The kidnapping of an Israeli soldier presents Israel's leaders with a terrible moral, legal, political, and strategic dilemma. Jewish law commands that ransom be paid for a captive unless the price may endanger the community. However, paying a ransom risks encouraging Israel's enemies to take more captives.

Imagine you are the prime minister of Israel. An Israeli soldier has been captured and is being held in Gaza. A terrorist group has informed you that the soldier will be released in exchange for Israel's release of a certain number of terrorists held in Israeli jails. The soldier's family and their supporters protest in front of your house every day, demanding that you bring their child home. The media publicizes the captive's plight and the suffering of his family.

At the same time, the families of the victims of the terrorists, who are now in jail, are sympathetic to the soldier's plight but encourage you not to release the terrorists. They ask, why is one soldier's life more valuable than those of their loved ones who died at the hands of terrorists?

What would you do?

example, Israel traded 1,150 prisoners for three soldiers. In 2004, Israel freed 430 Palestinian prisoners for the bodies of three soldiers and one civilian. In an effort to win the release of more incarcerated Palestinians, Hamas kidnapped nineteen-year-old Corporal Gilad Shalit on June 25, 2006. Hamas refused to allow anyone, including the Red Cross, to visit Shalit, and for years the only indication he was alive was a video released in October 2009. After years of unsuccessful negotiations to free Shalit, an agreement was finally reached in October 2011. Israel agreed to release 1,027 Palestinian prisoners in exchange for Shalit.

Israelis were filled with a mixture of elation and pain over the decision. While Israelis were overwhelmingly happy to see Shalit return home safely after 1,940 days of captivity, they were concerned that Palestinians who had committed heinous terror attacks might return to violence after their release. They also worried that the trade would encourage more kidnappings. Meanwhile, the parents of the victims of the terror attacks asked why the killers of their family members should be allowed to escape justice. The deal touched off a fierce debate over what the government should do in the event a soldier is kidnapped.

> My greatest wish for Israel is that someday it will be fully recognized as a country and no one will question its right to exist.
>
> MICHAL, AGE 19,
> WESTFIELD, NEW JERSEY

▲ Temple Mount at night, including Western Wall and Dome of the Rock, Jerusalem. The Western Wall (the Kotel) is the only remaining part of the retaining wall of the Second Temple. Beside it is the Temple Mount, a forty-acre plateau that is home to the Dome of the Rock and the Al-Aqsa Mosque.

▲ Concert at Sultan's Pool, Jerusalem. Although steeped in ancient history, Jerusalem has a vibrant cultural life. The Sultan's Pool was part of the water system of Jerusalem from the Roman period until the late Ottoman period. It is now used as a venue for concerts and festivals.

◄ Arab grilled-meat-stand vendor and Hasidic pedestrian, Jerusalem. Modern Jerusalem is a culturally diverse city; people from many different ethnic and religious groups live side by side.

Ethiopian man praying on promenade ▶
overlooking Jerusalem. Ethiopian Jews in Israel are referred to as Beta Israel and trace their roots to a tribe descended from King Solomon. In addition to Hebrew, many Israeli Ethiopians speak Amharic, one of the languages of Ethiopia.

◀ **Israeli soldiers at the Western Wall, Jerusalem.** Because military duty is compulsory for most Israelis, the army is an important rite of passage for young Israelis from all walks of life.

Worshipers at the Church of the Holy ▶
Sepulchre, Jerusalem. Located in the Old City of Jerusalem, the church is believed by many to be the place where Jesus was crucified and buried. It is an important pilgrimage destination for Christians from around the world.

◀ **Nubian Ibex, Ein Gedi Nature Reserve.** Located on the Dead Sea's western shore, Ein Gedi is a desert oasis and hiker's paradise, featuring beautiful foliage, waterfalls, exotic birds, and a range of wildlife, including hyraxes, foxes, ibex, and leopards.

▼ **Salt deposits in the Dead Sea.** The Dead Sea is the lowest place on earth, roughly thirteen hundred feet below sea level. It has the highest concentration of minerals in the world, and salt deposits saturate the water with therapeutic properties.

▲ **Ancient doorway, Safed.** The city of Safed in the Galilee features a warren of cobblestone streets that lead to many ancient synagogues. Safed is also home to many artists' studios.

Preserved aqueduct from ▶ the Roman period, along the coast of the Mediterranean Sea. Aqueducts built by the Romans carried water from springs on the Carmel Mountains to Caesarea. This feat of Roman engineering enabled drinking water to be brought into the city.

◀ **Baha'i gardens and Haifa panorama.** The port city of Haifa stretches from the shores of the Mediterranean up the slope of Mount Carmel. The city is populated by Arabs and Jews and is known as a model of peaceful coexistence. Haifa is the home of the Baha'i faith's world headquarters, featuring terraced gardens and a gold-domed shrine.

Bedouin market, ▶ **Be'er Sheva.** Be'er Sheva is a modern city of approximately 200,000 people and home to Ben-Gurion University; it is also the home of approximately 27,000 Bedouin, who still live a nomadic lifestyle.

▲ **Cliff overlooking the Ramon Crater, Negev.** The Ramon Crater is the largest of the three craters in the Negev desert. The Ramon Nature Reserve and the surrounding Negev mountains comprise the largest nature preserve in Israel and feature magnificent geological formations.

▲ **View of Jaffa from Tel Aviv.** Jaffa, one of the world's most ancient towns, was a fortified port city overlooking the Mediterranean. Because of its strategic location between Asia, Africa, and Europe, Jaffa was the target of conquerers throughout the ages. Today, Jaffa is a popular tourist destination, and its beautifully restored old quarter is filled with galleries, shops, and restaurants.

Outdoor café on Sheinkin Street, ▶
Tel Aviv. Tel Aviv is Israel's business and cultural center. It features an active street life with busy cafés, upscale restaurants, and trendy boutiques.

Harvesting bananas ▶ on a kibbutz. Agriculture is a major part of Israel's economy. Its banana industry is thriving; quality bananas are distributed throughout the country and are exported to Europe.

▼ Eilat hotel and promenade. Eilat lies on the coast of the Red Sea, at the southernmost tip of Israel. Featuring spectacular underwater preserves, bird watching, and beachfront hotels and nightclubs, Eilat is a popular vacation destination for Israelis and tourists from around the world.

CHAPTER THIRTEEN

ISRAEL LOOKS TO THE FUTURE

Although military moves such as Operation Cast Lead get most of the media attention, it is important to look beyond the headlines to better understand and analyze Israel's options for resolving the conflict with the Palestinians.

THREE OPTIONS

Israel's National Security Council has identified three principal options:

1. Annex the territories; that is, officially make the West Bank and Gaza Strip part of Israel;

169

2. Withdraw unilaterally; that is, evacuate territory without waiting for the Palestinians to make moves in exchange;

3. Negotiate a peace agreement.

Let's examine those options.

Annexing the Territories

More than four decades have passed since Israel took over the West Bank and Gaza Strip after the 1967 Six-Day War. At any time during those years, the Israeli government could have said that the West Bank and Gaza Strip were now officially part of Israel, but it has chosen not to take that step.

A major concern is that taking over the territories would affect the demography of Israel. The Israeli population is now 7.8 million, with a little less than six million Jews, but if Israel annexed the territories, approximately three million Palestinians would be added to the country, meaning the percentage of Jews in Israel would drop from 75 percent of the population to roughly 56 percent overnight.

Israel could potentially cease to be a Jewish state, since Israeli Arabs have a higher birthrate and could therefore become the majority. To prevent the loss of the Jewish majority, Israel could annex the territories but deny Palestinians the right to vote. However, denial of rights to a group of people would mean Israel would no longer be a democracy. Every Israeli leader has recognized this dilemma.

Withdrawing from Territories

In 2005 the Israeli government tried this option, withdrawing unilaterally from Gaza, hoping this step would lead to further peace efforts and help resolve the demographic problem. However, the withdrawal backfired when Hamas took over Gaza and used the territory as a base from which to attack Israel. The instability in the region created by the "Arab Spring" also highlights the potential danger if the situation in the areas Israel evacuates changes and becomes more hazardous. On the other hand, some believe that the current Palestinian leadership cannot or will not make peace, so the best way to end Israeli responsibility for the territories is to act unilaterally.

Negotiating an Agreement

Most Israelis prefer the third option—negotiating a peace agreement with the Palestinians. This would allow Israel to withdraw to secure and defensible borders that would incorporate most Jews living in settlements near the Green Line, and it would permit the Palestinians to establish a state in the remainder of the West Bank and Gaza Strip. If the Palestinians agreed to end the conflict with Israel permanently, the peoples of Israel and the new state of Palestine could live in peace and develop a wide range of mutually beneficial relationships in trade, tourism, and environmentalism.

Israel has been trying for many years to negotiate such an agreement, particularly through the Oslo Accords. Rabin hoped that Arafat would follow the lead of Egyptian president Anwar Sadat and negotiate a peace agreement with Israel. But after nine years, Israelis concluded that Arafat had not given up the dream of a Palestinian state replacing Israel.

After Arafat died, Israelis hoped his successor, Mahmoud Abbas, would be more willing to compromise. While Abbas has seemed more receptive to a deal, he has less control of the Palestinian leadership. Abbas lacks Arafat's popularity and clout among the Palestinian people and does not command the loyalty of the armed Palestinian militias. Consequently, Israelis are skeptical that he can deliver on promises he makes to Israel.

Prospects for negotiations have been severely hampered by the rise of Hamas, which won 2006 legislative elections among the Palestinians and seized control of the Gaza Strip in June 2007. Hamas states its commitment to Israel's destruction, and many countries in the world have labeled Hamas a terrorist organization, restricting negotiations and contact with the group. Hamas and Abbas's Fatah party have fought each other for power. Although they have periodically discussed a reconciliation, these efforts have failed. In 2003, the United Nations, the Russian Federation, the United States, and the

European Union formed the Quartet to work together to try to advance the peace process. The Quartet has shunned Hamas and said it cannot be a participant in negotiations unless it meets three conditions: recognizing Israel's right to exist, ending all terror, and agreeing to adhere to prior agreements signed by Israel and the Palestinians.

THE SETTLEMENT ISSUE

One of President Obama's priorities in 2009 was to negotiate a solution to the Palestinian-Israeli conflict. In a meeting with Israeli prime minister Netanyahu in May 2009, Obama called on Israel to freeze all settlement construction as a precondition for negotiations. Netanyahu agreed to an unprecedented ten-month freeze but refused to stop building in Jerusalem on grounds that it is Israel's capital and not part of the disputed territories. When Palestinian leaders saw that Obama could not force Netanyahu to adopt a total freeze, they began to question whether Obama was strong enough to force Israel to make the concessions they wanted.

This focus on the settlement issue had the unintended consequence of thwarting the prospects for negotiations. The Palestinians had never before insisted upon a settlement freeze as a precondition for negotiations. They had agreed to the Oslo Accords without insisting on a freeze, and, just before Obama took office, Prime Minister Ehud Olmert had met with Abbas thirty-five times to try to negotiate peace without a settlement freeze. Once Obama made it an issue, however, Abbas could not afford to look like he was demanding less than the US president.

When the Palestinian leader finally agreed to sit down for talks with Israel, he announced that he would continue to negotiate only if Israel imposed a complete and indefinite freeze. Netanyahu refused, arguing that Abbas had declined to talk during the ten-month freeze, so there was no reason to believe he would negotiate if the freeze was extended. Abbas walked out in September 2010, placing the negotiations in limbo. Netanyahu and Obama have repeatedly called for a return to negotiations, but Abbas has remained intransigent.

Look Closer

Because no Palestinian leader or group seems willing or able to negotiate with Israel, many Israelis say it is pointless to pursue that option. Some people believe the best alternative is unilateral withdrawal from the territories but not necessarily from all territory gained in the Six-Day War. Since that war, Israel's official policy has been that it is prepared to withdraw to the 1967 borders with modifications—meaning that Israel holds on to some parts of the West Bank and Jerusalem to ensure the nation's security.

People who favor a unilateral solution believe Israel should complete building the security fence to mark the new border and withdraw all Israelis to its side. The Palestinians would then be free to create an independent state on their side of the barrier. If they choose to live in peace, the fence could eventually be torn down or at least opened to trade, tourism, and exchanges of workers.

Few Israelis favor such a unilateral step now, following the painful experiences of the withdrawals from Lebanon and Gaza. In both cases, the territories Israel gave up became bases for launching terror attacks. Many Israelis express concern that the same thing could happen in the West Bank, and then the heart of the country—Tel Aviv, Jerusalem, and its international airport—would be within rocket range.

ARAB SPRING

The situation became more complicated in the spring of 2011. The "Arab Spring" began with revolts across the Middle East. As citizens fought for democracy against authoritarian rulers, upheavals in Tunisia, Egypt, Libya, Syria, Yemen, and some of the Persian Gulf states threatened to destabilize the entire region. The fate of these countries is still uncertain, and it may be years before it becomes clear what types of regimes will emerge.

In the meantime, this instability has created new security concerns for Israel. Long-time Egyptian president, Hosni Mubarak, had kept the Israel-Egypt Peace Treaty intact for more than thirty years. The fall of his regime, with no clear successor on the horizon, has raised fears that radical Islamists could take over Egypt and abrogate the treaty. If this occurs, Israel would face the region's largest, best-trained, and American-armed military.

PALESTINIANS BID FOR STATEHOOD

Despite the turmoil all around Israel, Netanyahu continued to call for direct negotiations to resolve all outstanding issues with the Palestinians. At the same time, the Palestinians launched their own unilateral bid to achieve statehood. Defying the United States and other Western countries, the Palestinian Authority decided in September 2011 to ask the UN Security Council to recognize an independent state of Palestine based on the 1967 borders with East Jerusalem as its capital. Israel and its supporters argued that statehood could be achieved only through face-to-face talks, in which both sides agreed on future borders as well as the future of Jerusalem, refugees, and settlements. The United States threatened to veto the UN resolution, effectively assuring the proposal would not be adopted. As the Palestinians continued to lobby other nations to support its UN bid, the United States resumed its push for the two sides to negotiate, and the Quartet laid out a timetable for resolving outstanding issues and reaching a final agreement.

> " My greatest wish for Israel is for it to improve its relations with surrounding countries. My greatest hope is that my generation is more tolerant than the generations preceding it and that the generation to follow is more tolerant than my own. "
>
> SARAH, AGE 16,
> MADISON, CONNECTICUT

While the situation may seem bleak or even hopeless, it is important to remember that it took thirty years for Israel to achieve peace with Egypt and another fifteen years before it signed a treaty with Jordan. The success of those arrangements has proved that Israel can live in peace with its neighbors after agreements have been reached. The treaties with Egypt and Jordan offer hope that a broader peace is possible, in which all the countries of the Middle East enjoy normal political, economic, and personal relations.

Think about It

If Israel chooses to annex the West Bank, what rights should it give to Palestinians living there?

???

ISRAEL MATTERS TO AMERICA
Ideological Affinities

Most polls show that Americans believe Israel is an important ally of the United States and favor close ties between the two countries. This affinity goes back decades and is a result of American perceptions that Israelis share their values and interests. Israelis have always shared the American belief that people are a nation's greatest resource. Though it is a small country, Israel has proven that people can make a difference by building a modern nation out of what literally were malarial swamps and desert.

Like the United States, Israel is also a nation of immigrants. Newcomers to Israel, just like immigrants to America, have tried to make better lives for themselves and their children. Some have arrived from Western countries and have had to adapt to a new culture. Others have come from relatively undeveloped societies like Ethiopia or Yemen; they arrived with virtually no possessions, education, or training and have become productive contributors to Israeli society.

Israel's economy shares similarities with America's. In its early years, Israel combined capitalism with socialism along the British model. The economic difficulties Israel has experienced—created largely in the aftermath of the Yom Kippur War by increased oil prices and the need to spend a disproportionate share of its gross national product on defense—have led to a gradual movement toward a free-market economy. Even with its economic and security challenges, Israel has had an extraordinary rate of economic growth for most of its history.

> "The security of Israel matters to me because I want my kids, my grandkids, and my great-grandkids to visit the place I call home. Without a secure country, my future family may not have the opportunity to see or live in the land of the Jewish people."
>
> ALEX, AGE 17,
> PORTLAND, OREGON

Americans' affinity for Israel also stems from shared aspirations for a democratic society. Though Israelis live in a region dominated by autocracies, they have a commitment to democracy no less passionate than that of Americans. This commitment to freedom and the civil rights Americans hold dear—freedom of speech, freedom of assembly, freedom of religion, women's rights, gay rights—distinguishes Israel from its neighbors and from America's Arab allies.

Israelis also share Americans' passion for education; Israel boasts world-class universities and research institutes, and has achieved striking scientific and medical advances. Not surprisingly, Israeli and American educational institutions engaged in a variety of cooperative activities and joint projects have produced many innovations that benefit both nations.

STRAIGHT from the Source

"America's commitment to Israel's security flows from a deeper place—and that's the values we share. As two people who struggled to win our freedom against overwhelming odds, we understand that preserving the security for which our forefathers—and foremothers—fought must be the work of every generation. As two vibrant democracies, we recognize that the liberties and freedoms we cherish must be constantly nurtured. And as the nation that recognized the State of Israel moments after its independence, we have a profound commitment to its survival as a strong, secure homeland for the Jewish people."

– PRESIDENT BARACK OBAMA, AIPAC POLICY CONFERENCE, MAY 22, 2011

Geopolitical Interests

Stability in the Middle East is of primary importance to US interests. Instability in the region can threaten world oil supplies, provide fertile ground for terrorists, and provoke conflicts involving many nations. Radical Islamic groups opposed to US policies and committed to spreading their extremist views in an effort to create a new Islamic empire also pose a threat to the United States and its allies.

The United States considers Israel a key ally and provides billions of dollars in foreign aid to help Israel defend itself and prevent terrorism. US aid also goes to many Arab countries and advocacy groups, and the United States often urges Israel to take more steps to ensure fair treatment of the Palestinians and Israeli Arabs within its borders.

The United States has long been involved in trying to negotiate peace between Israel and its neighbors, from the shuttle diplomacy of Henry Kissinger to efforts made by Presidents George W. Bush and Bill Clinton.

The US-Israel alliance is based on mutual benefit. In the months following September 11, 2001, Israel was in the position of offering its guidance and support to America. Israeli security experts gave advice to American agencies on how they could prevent another terrorist attack in the United States.

Strategic Interests

Israel continues to play a role in protecting American interests in the region, and strategic cooperation has continued to evolve to the point where a de facto alliance now exists. Israeli and American soldiers regularly train and conduct exercises together. Israeli weapons systems also are used by US forces. The two countries have cooperated in fighting terrorism for many years and have worked even more closely since September 11. Israeli security experts routinely work with American agencies to develop technology, strategies, and information to prevent terrorist attacks in the United States.

While Israel and America are bound together by security interests, the countries also engage in programs related to their shared values. These shared-value initiatives cover a broad range of areas such as the environment, energy, space, occupational safety, and health. It is common for mayors, governors, and state and federal legislators to visit Israel to share knowledge and best practices.

Americans and Israelis have always had relationships at the state and local level, and a milestone in formalizing these contacts occurred in 1985 when the Texas-Israel Exchange was created to promote mutually beneficial projects between the Texas Department of Agriculture and Israel's Ministry of Agriculture. Since then, at least thirty-three other states and the District of Columbia have signed agreements with Israel to increase cooperation in trade, tourism, research, culture, and other activities of particular interest to individual states. It has now become routine for governors to lead delegations of

Faces of Israel

Brad spent a semester abroad studying in England. Though he grew up with a strong Jewish identity, he wasn't interested enough in Israel to go to school there and actually visited twenty-five European countries and Egypt before deciding to make Israel his last stop. He went to the Western Wall and was approached by a man in a dark suit and black hat he assumed was an ultra-Orthodox Jew. The man asked Brad in perfect English if he had the time, and Brad answered. The man then struck up a conversation. "You're from America? Where?" Brad answered that he was from California, and the man, who introduced himself as a rabbi, asked if Brad was interested in philosophy. Brad said yes and thought the rabbi was going to invite him to a lecture. Instead, the rabbi said, "Come with me," and the next thing Brad knew he had a room in a yeshiva. Brad spent a week there, enjoying free room and board and a choice of classes. He found the yeshiva intellectually stimulating, and Brad considered becoming more observant. This experience was transformative for him, and he has returned to Israel at least once a year for over thirty years.

business leaders, educators, and cultural affairs officials to Israel and for state agencies and institutions to initiate joint projects.

The first free trade agreement signed by the United States was with Israel in 1985; it served as the model for others the United States signed with Canada, Jordan, and Mexico, among other countries. The volume of trade between the two countries increased nearly 1,000 percent and reached a total value of more than $32 billion in 2010.

In addition, more than ten thousand US companies do business in Israel or with Israeli counterparts. Both the United States and Israel share an entrepreneurial vision, and the exchange of talent and ideas is important for innovative companies in both countries. Many companies, including high-tech giants such as Motorola, Intel, and Microsoft, have built plants in Israel and draw upon Israel's extraordinary pool of technical talent.

ISRAEL'S DESIRE

Israel has faced great challenges over the past six decades and still confronts enemies who seek its destruction. In consistently overcoming these challenges, the country has not only survived but thrived.

Many challenges remain, both external and internal, and no one should be surprised that such a young country still has obstacles to overcome. Israelis dream of the day when they will live in peace with their neighbors and when all their energies can be devoted to building a better nation for themselves and their children.

ISRAEL'S SIGNIFICANCE TO THE WORLD

Israel's story speaks to humanitarian principles worldwide. For example, Israel matters to people seeking a haven. As a nation of immigrants, its story offers hope for people around the world who are in exile. For Jews, Israel is the one place that will offer them automatic citizenship and welcome them unconditionally. Israel matters to people of other faiths and cultures seeking freedom as

> " Israel is a spiritual icon, providing religious refuge and symbolism to people around the world. It is also a lead innovator in medicine and technology. "
>
> GABRIELLE, AGE 19, AMBLER, PENNSYLVANIA

well, such as refugees from Sudan and Vietnam, and gay Palestinians, all of whom have fled their homes and found safety in Israel.

Israel matters on religious grounds. Israel is the spiritual home to the world's three major religions. Christians venerate it as the birthplace of Jesus, the site of his miracles, and the place where they believe the Messiah will return. Israel matters to Muslims who maintain their third holiest shrine, the Al-Aqsa Mosque, on the Temple Mount. And Jews believe Israel is their ancient homeland, the Promised Land, where King David and his successors ruled and Solomon's Temple once stood. People of all faiths—Jews, Christians, Muslims, Baha'is, and others—are free to practice their religions in Israel.

Israel is a beacon for people who seek to live in freedom and enjoy the fruits of democracy. It is a place that believes in freedom of speech, religion, assembly, and the press. Israel matters to anyone who believes in the importance of individual rights as well as human rights.

Historically, Israel matters to people who treasure the past and wish to walk in the footsteps of figures from the Bible, and from Roman, Greek, Ottoman, Islamic, and Jewish history. The history of past civilizations that lived on this small patch of land in the Middle East is preserved, from the town of Megiddo dating back five thousand years, to the works of Israel's modern artists exhibited at the Israel Museum. The juxtaposition of ancient and modern contributes to Israel's thriving culture, which inspires people all over the world.

MAKING A CONNECTION TO ISRAEL

A reader of this book may feel a connection to Israel for one of the reasons mentioned above, or maybe Israel is too abstract right now, a faraway place that is only familiar from the news, the Bible, or from discussions with friends and family. One's feelings may be conflicted: it is possible to admire some aspects of

Israel's history and culture, yet feel uncomfortable with particular policies. If a reader is an observant Jew, he or she may view Israel as a fountain of spirituality. Another reader may feel connected to Israel because of a cultural or ethnic affinity to Israelis or to fellow Jews. Wherever one finds him- or herself on this spectrum, we are all participants in the conversation about Israel's past, its present, and its prospects for the future. This book is a starting place. There is much more to read and explore—the conversation about Israel is never-ending, passionate, and meaningful, and it always matters.

> My biggest fear is that Israel will not exist for my children or my children's children. Hillel once said, 'If not now when?' This is so important! Israel is at a do-or-die state every day, and without the support of teens like me, who knows what will happen in the future? My fellow teens and I are the future of the world and the future of Israel. Israel's fate lies in our hands.
>
> NATALIE, AGE 16, BLOOMFIELD, MICHIGAN

ACT ON IT

DISCUSSION QUESTIONS AND SUGGESTED ACTIVITIES

1. Israel is often portrayed as a place of conflict. Craft a publicity campaign, creating slogans, fact sheets, advertisements, or videos to show a more positive side of Israel.

2. Contact an Israeli high school and start an internet-based project to compare data about your country with Israel. This can be personal, and may include a comparison of young peoples' lives (for example: post-high school plans, military service, popular career choices, use of technology), or more general (for example: compare cost-of-living statistics, average family size, home ownership, etc.).

3. Judaism, Christianity, and Islam all recognize and honor certain Jewish patriarchs and prophets. Research how each of the religions views figures such as Abraham, Moses, David, and Daniel. What are the similarities taught by each faith about these men? What are the differences?

4. Write a creative short story, play, or poem based on a Russian-Jewish family who fled to Israel to escape persecution.

5. Create a plan for a kibbutz in your classroom or neighborhood. How would you divide responsibilities? How would you enforce the rules?

6. Draft a report for the United Nations on what to do to resolve the conflicting claims of Jews and Arabs in pre-1948 Palestine.

7. Choose a country to represent at the United Nations and cast your vote for whether pre-1948 Palestine should be divided into Jewish and Arab states or whether the land should be reserved for only one group. If you want to give the land to one group, who should receive it? Explain the reasons for your vote. Do you have another idea for how to resolve the conflict?

8. Look at a map of Palestine as it existed in 1947. How would you have divided the land between Palestinian Arabs and Jews?

9. Compare the Israeli Declaration of Independence to the US Declaration of Independence. How are they alike? How are they different?

10. Prepare a proposal about Palestinian resettlement that you could have presented to the United Nations in 1948 after Israel's War of Indpendence. How can these Palestinians be resettled? Where?

11. Create multiple "political parties" in your class and hold an election similar to the parliamentary elections in Israel. Does any one group win a majority? How would you form coalitions in order to achieve a majority?

12. Americans believe that you can't have separate school systems that are equal. Israelis believe that Jews (secular and religious, respectively) and Arabs can and should have separate elementary educations. Debate the merits of the two systems.

13. Write a new UN resolution for Middle East peace after the Six-Day War.

14. Plan a debate about the rights of Palestinians in the West Bank and Gaza Strip. Should they be given the same rights as Israeli Arabs? Should they be given independence and self-government?

15. Discuss security measures that will discourage terrorist attacks in a variety of situations, such as travel, sporting events, and in everyday places such as schools and markets.

16. Choose one key issue the Oslo Accords left unresolved and offer solutions to resolve it.

17. Imagine it is 1973. Draft a statement for the president of the United States to read to the American people explaining his decision to send arms to Israel.

18. Using a detailed map of Israel and the West Bank, draw where you believe the borders of Israel and Palestine should be, given Israeli security concerns and Palestinian demands.

19. Put together an invitation list for an international conference to promote peace in the Middle East. Whom would you invite and how would you convince them to attend?

20. Pretend that you are in charge of a group of soldiers preparing to go into a crowded neighborhood in the Gaza Strip. You know that Hamas members with bomb-making materials are in a house somewhere on the block, but you also know that many innocent civilians live there. What instructions would you give your group about the assignment?

21. You are the newly elected president of the United States. You have watched the last two presidents struggle as they tried and failed to help broker a final deal between Israel and Palestinian leaders. How will you approach this issue?

22. Imagine you have been invited to facilitate a retreat at which Israeli and Palestinian teenagers are working together to come up with some solutions for achieving peace among their communities. What activities would you propose to make this gathering meaningful and effective? What challenges would you face and how would you work through them?

23. You are an ordinary Israeli citizen living in Tel Aviv. You know your country would be better off if it could live in peace. What steps can you take to help that happen?

24. Terrorists fire rockets from the Gaza Strip into southern Israel. While this region is less populated, citizens are affected. What would you advise the Israeli prime minister to do in response? And if the rockets were fired from the West Bank and landed in Jerusalem, would your advice be the same?

25. Israelis and Americans are interested in protecting the environment. Find an Israeli school with which you can communicate and develop a joint project. Monitor some aspect of the local environment or compare the use of solar energy in Israel with its use in the United States.

GLOSSARY

Aliyah: Literally "ascent" in Hebrew. This term is applied to Jews moving to Israel. The term also refers to a wave of immigration, when thousands of Jews moved to Israel in a short period of time.

Allah: Arabic term for God. Arabs frequently use the word *inshallah*, meaning "if God wills."

Balfour Declaration: Statement issued by the British government in 1917 recognizing the Jewish people's right to a national home in the Land of Israel. It was named for Lord Balfour, then foreign secretary, who signed it on Britain's behalf.

Bedouin: Nomadic Arabs who originally inhabited desert areas of the Middle East and northern Africa and later began to move to other parts of the region. Most Bedouin today are settled, and many live in urban settings. Virtually all are Muslims.

Circassians: Located in various areas of the Middle East, in Israel they represent a small community of approximately three thousand people concentrated in two northern villages. Circassians are Sunni Muslims, although they share neither the Arab origin nor the cultural background of the larger Islamic community.

While maintaining a distinct ethnic identity, they participate in Israel's economic and national affairs without assimilating into either Jewish society or the general Muslim community.

Crusades: A series of military campaigns fought by Western European Christians in an effort to recapture the Holy Land from the Muslims. The First Crusade took place from 1095 to 1099; the ninth and final crusade in the Middle East took place from 1271 to 1272. The word was later used to describe Christian wars against non-Christians.

Desalination: A process that removes salt from seawater, making the water suitable for drinking, washing, and agricultural purposes.

Dhimma: "Writ of protection." Muslims held special respect for Jews and Christians, whom they called "People of the Book," and accepted Moses and Jesus as prophets. Jews and Christians therefore were given special status in Muslim countries as protected persons. The classification of *dhimma* was introduced, giving the dhimmis certain rights denied other minorities and conquered peoples, but which still made clear these respected groups were viewed as inferior to Muslims.

Diaspora: From the Greek word for "dispersion." Jews use the term to refer to the period when they were exiled from Israel. The term is also used to describe all the places outside Israel in which Jews live.

Druze: A Muslim sect that lives primarily in Lebanon, southern Syria, and northern Israel. The basis of the Druze religion is the belief that at various times God has been divinely incarnated in a living person and that his last, and final, such incarnation was al-Hakim, the sixth Fatimid caliph, who announced himself in Cairo in about 1016. The Druze believe in one God but do not pray in a mosque and are secretive about the tenets of their religion.

Green Line: The borderline between Israel and the West Bank territories that were captured in the 1967 Six-Day War.

Haganah: A clandestine Jewish military defense force in Palestine under the British Mandate, which eventually evolved into the Israel Defense Forces.

Hamas: Arabic acronym for the Islamic Resistance Movement, a fundamentalist Palestinian group that rejects all discussion of peace with Israel. Hamas has been responsible for many terrorist attacks against Israeli civilians and Palestinian collaborators with Israel.

Hezbollah: Arabic for "Party of God." The group is an Iranian- and Syrian-backed Islamic fundamentalist organization based in predominantly Shiite areas of southern Lebanon. It is the dominant political power in the country and is known for providing social services to Shiites in the country. It also has engaged in terror attacks on Israeli soldiers and civilians, Jews outside Israel, and Americans, and the group maintains an internal militia inside Lebanon.

Histadrut: Jewish Labor Federation. Created in 1920 as a trade union to organize the economic activities of Jewish workers. Histadrut's goals are to ensure employment and job security for all.

Intifada: Literally "shaking off" and metaphorically "uprising" in Arabic. The term has been used to refer to two Palestinian uprisings against Israeli occupation. The first began in December 1987 and the second in September 2000.

Irgun: National Military Organization. Known as the Etzel, this underground Jewish organization in Palestine was founded in 1931 to fight against the Arabs and the British.

Jihad: From the Arabic verb *jahada*, "exerted"; commonly rendered as "holy war." Though jihad has become associated with violence because Islamic terrorists have claimed they act as part of a jihad against Israel and the West, the fight against nonbelievers may also be pursued through peaceful means.

Judea and Judah: Both terms are used for the southern part of historic Palestine that included the cities of Jerusalem, Hebron, and Bethlehem. When the Romans conquered the Jewish kingdom, they divided Palestine into three administrative areas: Judea, Galilee, and Samaria. Judea is the Roman rendering of the Hebrew Yehuda (Judah). The word *Jew* comes from the Latin *Judaeus*, meaning "an inhabitant of Judea."

Judea and Samaria: Names that have long been used for the regions west of the Jordan River. Since Menachem Begin's time, at least, these geographic references have acquired political meaning. People who refer to Judea and Samaria in political debate usually believe these territories are part of Israel and should remain so. Those who refer to the area simply as the West Bank tend to take the opposite view.

Kibbutz (plural, kibbutzim): Communal settlement in modern Israel. Originally *kibbutzim* focused on agriculture, but many of them are now engaged in a variety of activities, including tourism, high-tech ventures, and other industries. Although today their precise organization varies, classically *kibbutzim* were an attempt to found a new type of community with shared dining halls, child-rearing facilities, and finances.

Knesset: Israel's Parliament. The Knesset has 120 members elected through a system of proportional representation. Parties choose their own lists of candidates, who are allotted seats based on the proportion of the vote the parties receive in an election. For example, if a party wins enough votes to qualify for six seats in the Knesset, the first six people on the party list become members.

Koran: From the Arabic *kara'a*, which means "read." This book contains the divine revelations given to Muhammad through the angel Gabriel that were compiled by Muhammad's followers after his death. Because God is believed to be the author, the Koran is considered infallible. The Sharia (Arabic for "the way") is the body of laws that regulate Muslim life, some of which appear explicitly in the Koran. These rules are believed to be an expression of God's will, but they are also subject to the interpretation of Islamic scholars.

Kosher: Observance of traditional Jewish dietary laws based on the Bible and rabbinic interpretations.

Labor Party: Israeli political party formed by the union of three left-of-center socialist parties. Labor (under different names) held power from 1948 to 1977, dominating Israeli public and political life. Labor continues to be one of the major political parties in Israel.

Likud Party: Israeli political party whose roots can be traced back to Ze'ev (Vladimir) Jabotinsky; it is associated with right-of-center, nationalist, free-market policies.

Maccabees: The family of Mattathias became known as the Maccabees, from the Hebrew word for "hammer," because they were said to strike hammer blows against their enemies. The Maccabees are referenced in the story of Hanukkah.

Mandate: System created by the League of Nations to allow member nations to govern former German colonies and other conquered lands, including those once part of the Ottoman Empire.

Messiah: From the Hebrew word *Mashi'ach*, meaning "one who is anointed." "Jesus Christ" is Greek for "Joshua the Messiah." Jews and Christians have different conceptions of the Messiah. The Jewish view of the Messiah is that of an earthly redeemer, instructed by God to bring justice and peace to the world. The Christian understanding of the Messiah is that of the divine redeemer, manifesting God's presence on earth.

Middle East: Sometimes referred to as the Near East; an area of southwestern Asia and northern Africa that stretches from the Mediterranean Sea to Pakistan and includes the Arabian Peninsula. The total population of these nations is more than 400 million. The term sometimes excludes the Arab countries of North Africa between Morocco in the west and Libya in the east, an area that has also been called the Maghreb.

Moshav: A cooperative institution in Israel similar to a kibbutz. On a moshav, however, farms are owned by individuals who keep the profits from their labors, while members share the cost of purchasing supplies and market-ing what they produce.

Mossad: The Israeli government's intelligence agency. Like the CIA, the Mossad uses agents to collect intelligence, conduct covert operations, and fight terrorism. Its primary focus is on terrorist organizations and the Arab/Muslim nations in the Middle East.

Mufti: An expert who is responsible for interpreting Muslim law, held in high esteem by the population. The mufti's opinion is expressed in a document called a fatwa. The mufti of Jerusalem, Haj Amin al-Husseini, played a critical role in incit-ing the Palestinian Arabs against the Jews and British during the Mandate period.

OPEC: Acronym for the Organization of the Petroleum Exporting Countries. OPEC was founded in 1960 when the oil-producing nations of Iran, Iraq, Kuwait, Saudi Arabia, and Venezuela joined together to try to control oil prices by restricting the supply available on the market. The five founding members were later joined by Qatar, Indonesia, Libya, United Arab Emirates, Algeria, Nigeria, Ecuador, Angola, and Gabon. Today, OPEC continues to influence the price of oil by regulating the amount each country produces. However, its influ-ence is partly blunted by the policies of other oil producers that are not part of OPEC, such as the United States, Mexico, Norway, and Russia.

Orthodox Judaism: Characterized by allegiance to a traditional inter-pretation and strict observance of the laws in the Torah as interpreted in the Talmud and other rabbinic writings. Orthodox Jews regard the Torah and its rabbinic interpretations as divinely revealed.

Palestine Liberation Organization (PLO): Umbrella organiza-tion whose dominant group is Fatah but that includes other Palestinian fac-tions such as the Popular Front for the Liberation of Palestine and the Democratic Front for the Liberation of Palestine. The PLO was founded in 1964 at the Cairo Summit. It was originally controlled by the Arab states, but after the 1967 Six-Day War, the Palestinians took control of the organization, which was led by Yasser Arafat until his death in 2004. Today, the Fatah faction controls only the West Bank. Hamas, which is not a member of the PLO, rules Gaza.

Palmach: An abbreviation for the Hebrew P'lugot Mahaz, which means "shock companies." The Palmach was an elite strike force within the Haganah.

Pogrom: An organized attack on a minority group in which people are murdered and their property destroyed. The term is usually applied to the massacre of Jews, particularly a series of murderous attacks that took place in Russia in the 1880s and the decades that followed.

Prophets: In Judaism, prophets are believed to be individuals chosen by God to disclose God's will and to arouse the people to repentance and observance of God's laws.

Quartet: An international committee consisting of representatives from the United States, the European Union, Russia, and the United Nations formed in 2003 to address the problems of the Israeli-Palestinian dispute.

Sanhedrin: Jewish court; were located in every city in ancient Judea. The Great Sanhedrin was a kind of Supreme Court that had 71 members and met in the Temple in Jerusalem. This was the highest religious and legal authority in Jewish life.

Self-determination: The principle that a people should be free to determine its own political status.

Semite: First used in the late eighteenth century for those who descended from Noah's son Shem. Today, it commonly identifies people who speak a Semitic language. Arabs sometimes claim they cannot be anti-Semitic (a term coined in Germany in 1879) because they, too, are Semites; however, anti-Semitism refers specifically to hatred of or discrimination against Jews.

Shiites: Second-largest Muslim sect behind the Sunnis. The divide between Sunni and Shiite Muslims stems from the early days of Islam and arguments over Muhammad's successors. Iran is the only nation with an overwhelming Shiite majority, but Iraq, Lebanon, and Bahrain have large Shiite communities.

Shuttle diplomacy: A diplomatic tactic in which a designated representative travels back and forth between parties that do not want to talk to each other in an effort to find common ground. The term was first used to describe US secretary of state Henry Kissinger's role after the October 1973 war between Israel and Arab states, especially Egypt and Syria. The most notable shuttles were aimed at convincing Israel and Egypt to reach agreements that would lead to an Israeli withdrawal from territories it captured in 1967 in exchange for Egyptian concessions. Two interim agreements were actually achieved. In addition, Kissinger dramatically negotiated a Syrian-Israeli disengagement accord in May 1974.

Sunnis: Largest group of Muslims. Sunnis accept the Islamic tradition and the legitimate authority of the caliphs as Muhammad's successors.

Temple Mount: An area of thirty-seven acres on Mount Moriah on which the Jewish Temple was built around 950 BCE. The Temple was destroyed in 586 BCE by the Babylonians and rebuilt seventy years later. It was razed by the Romans in 70 CE. The Muslims subsequently built the Dome of the Rock on the Temple Mount in 691 and added the Al-Aqsa mosque twenty years later.

Terrorism: The unlawful use of violence and threats to intimidate or coerce a government or its civilian population, especially for political purposes.

Theocracy: From the Greek *theokratia*, meaning "government by a god." In a theocracy, the country views God as the source of all law and legitimacy and often allows religious authorities to interpret the laws.

Torah: In Hebrew "teaching" or "instruction." Torah is sometimes used to describe all of Jewish tradition, but the term usually refers specifically to the Pentateuch, or the first five books of the Bible: Genesis, Exodus, Leviticus, Numbers, and Deuteronomy.

West Bank: The territory west of the River Jordan that Israel captured from Jordan in 1967. This area includes the territories known as Judea and Samaria in biblical times and was the region where the Jews actually lived in that period.

Yiddish: A language that uses the same alphabet as Hebrew but is a blend of Hebrew and several European languages, primarily German.

Yishuv: The Jewish community of Palestine prior to 1948.

Zealots: Comes from the Greek word meaning "enthusiastic." This term is used to describe a person who exhibits great enthusiasm and dedication to a cause. The word specifically refers to an early Jewish group that fought bitterly for Jewish independence from the Roman Empire.

Zionism: Coined by an Austrian journalist, Nathan Birnbaum, in 1890; the term is derived from Zion, the original name of the Jebusite stronghold in Jerusalem. Zion became a symbol for Jerusalem during the reign of King David. The goal of Zionism is the political and spiritual renewal of the Jewish people in its ancestral homeland, and a Zionist is someone who supports this objective.

TIMELINE

EARLY JEWISH HISTORY

1700 BCE	Famine forces Israelites to migrate to Egypt
1250-1200 BCE	Exodus from Egypt, entry into Canaan
1030-1010 BCE	Reign of King Saul
1010-970 BCE	Reign of King David; Jerusalem becomes capital
970-931 BCE	Reign of King Solomon, First Temple
931 BCE	Secession of Northern Kingdom (Israel) from Southern Kingdom (Judah)
722-721 BCE	Assyrians destroy Israel, ten tribes exiled
587-586 BCE	Judah and First Temple destroyed, Babylonian exile
538 BCE	Edict of Cyrus, first return from exile
520-515 BCE	Second Temple built
333-331 BCE	Alexander the Great conquers Palestine
166-160 BCE	Maccabean revolt
142-129 BCE	Jewish autonomy under Hasmoneans

THE RISE OF CHRISTIANITY

63 BCE	Rome annexes Palestine
37-4 BCE	Herod the Great, king of Judea

4 BCE-30 CE	Jesus
36-64 CE	Paul the Apostle
50-125 CE	New Testament writings
66-73 CE	Great Revolt against Rome
70 CE	Destruction of Jerusalem and the Second Temple
73 CE	Last stand of Jews at Masada
132-135 CE	Bar-Kokhba Revolt
200 CE	Mishnah (Oral Law) compiled and edited
312-313 CE	Constantine embraces Christianity
380-391 CE	Christianity becomes religion of Roman Empire

ISLAM BECOMES AN EMPIRE

570	Muhammad's birth
622	Hegira
638	Jews permitted by Muslims to return to Jerusalem
691	Dome of the Rock built in Jerusalem
950-1150	Golden Age of Spanish Jewry
1099	Crusaders capture Jerusalem
1187	Saladin recaptures Jerusalem from the Crusaders
1300s	Rise of Ottoman Muslim Dynasty in Turkey
1520-1566	Suleiman the Magnificent rules

FIRST ALIYAH

1881	Start of mass migrations of Eastern European Jews
1882-1903	First Aliyah to Israel, mainly from Russia
1896	Theodor Herzl publishes *The Jewish State*
1897	First Zionist Congress convened by Herzl in Basel, Switzerland; World Zionist Organization founded
1904-1914	Second Aliyah, mainly from Russia and Poland
1909	First kibbutz, Degania, founded in Israel
1914-1918	World War I

| 1916 | Start of Arab revolt against Ottoman Turkish rule |
| 1917 | Four hundred years of Ottoman rule ended by British conquest |

BALFOUR DECLARATION AND MANDATORY PERIOD

1917	Balfour Declaration recognizes the right of Jews to a Jewish national home in Palestine
1919-1923	Third Aliyah, mainly from Russia
1922	Great Britain grants Mandate for Palestine by League of Nations
1922	Transjordan boundaries set
1924-1932	Fourth Aliyah, mainly from Poland
1933-1939	Fifth Aliyah, mainly from Germany
1933	Adolf Hitler becomes chancellor of Germany
1936-1939	Anti-Jewish riots instigated by Arab militants in Palestine
1939	Jewish immigration severely limited by British White Paper
1939-1945	World War II
1945	League of Arab States formed in Cairo
1947	The *Exodus 1947* sails to Palestine and is denied entry
1947	United Nations proposes the establishment of Arab and Jewish states in Palestine

THE BIRTH OF MODERN ISRAEL

1948	End of British Mandate; Declaration of Independence of the State of Israel
1948	Israel invaded by five Arab states
1948-1949	Israeli War of Independence
1948-1952	Mass immigration to Israel from Europe and Arab countries
1949	Armistice agreements signed with Egypt, Jordan, Syria, Lebanon
1949	Jerusalem divided under Israeli and Jordanian rule
1949	First Knesset elected
1951	King Abdullah of Jordan is assassinated
1952-1954	Egyptian republic proclaimed; Nasser takes over
1953	King Hussein officially assumes the throne in Jordan

1956	Suez War
1963	David Ben-Gurion resigns as Israeli prime minister, replaced by Levi Eshkol
1964	Palestine Liberation Organization (PLO) is established

SIX-DAY WAR THROUGH 1984

1967	Six-Day War
1967	UN Security Council adopts Resolution 242
1969-1970	Egypt's War of Attrition against Israel
1970	King Hussein's troops expel rebellious Palestinians backed by Syria (Black September)
1971	Hafez al-Assad seizes power in Syria
1972	Eleven Israeli athletes murdered by PLO at Munich Olympic Games
1973	Yom Kippur War
1974	Golda Meir's government resigns; Yitzhak Rabin becomes prime minister of Israel
1976	Israel mounts rescue of hostages in Entebbe, Uganda
1977	Likud forms government, ending twenty-nine years of Labor rule
1977	Egyptian president Anwar Sadat visits Jerusalem
1978	Camp David Accords
1979	Israel-Egypt Peace Treaty signed
1981	Israeli air force destroys Iraqi nuclear reactor
1981	Egyptian president Anwar Sadat assassinated; Hosni Mubarak succeeds him
1982	Israel's three-stage withdrawal from Sinai completed
1982	Israeli invasion removes PLO leadership from Lebanon
1983	Menachem Begin abruptly resigns as Israel's prime minister
1984	Operation Moses, immigration of Jews from Ethiopia

FIRST INTIFADA THROUGH 2000

1987	First Intifada begins
1989	Start of mass immigration of Jews from former Soviet Union
1991	Israel hit by Iraqi Scud missiles during the Gulf War

1991	Middle East peace conference convenes in Madrid
1991	Operation Solomon, airlift of Jews from Ethiopia
1993	Oslo Accords signed by Israel and PLO
1994	Implementation of Palestinian self-government in Gaza Strip and Jericho area
1994	Israel-Jordan Peace Treaty signed
1994	Rabin, Peres, Arafat awarded Nobel Peace Prize
1995	Oslo II provides removal of Israeli troops from all key Palestinian towns in the West Bank
1995	Prime Minister Yitzhak Rabin assassinated at peace rally
1995	Shimon Peres becomes prime minister
1996	Benjamin Netanyahu wins first direct election for prime minister
1997	Agreement reached for Israeli withdrawal from Hebron in the West Bank
1998	Wye River Plantation talks; Israel agrees to additional withdrawal from West Bank
1999	Jordan's King Hussein dies, is succeeded by son Abdullah
1999	Ehud Barak elected prime minister of Israel
2000	Israel withdraws unilaterally from Lebanon
2000	Syrian president Hafez al-Assad dies in June, following talks with Israel; succeeded by son Bashar
2000	President Bill Clinton, Ehud Barak, and Yasser Arafat fail to reach agreement on Israeli-Palestinian settlement

SECOND INTIFADA THROUGH 2007

2000	Second Intifada begins
2000	Prime Minister Barak resigns
2001	Ariel Sharon elected prime minister of Israel
2002	President Bush calls for Arafat to be replaced; lays out plan for a provisional Palestinian state
2003	"Quartet" announces road map designed to facilitate Israeli-Palestinian settlement
2004	Sharon affirms plan to withdraw from Gaza
2004	Yasser Arafat dies in Paris

2005	Mahmoud Abbas elected president of Palestinian Authority
2005	Withdrawal from Gaza completed
2005	Sharon resigns from Likud Party, creates centrist Kadima party
2006	Sharon suffers severe stroke and falls into coma; Ehud Olmert assumes role of acting prime minister
2006	Hamas wins majority in Palestinian Authority general elections
2006	Kadima party wins election; Ehud Olmert is prime minister
2006	Hezbollah in Lebanon; month-long war begins
2007	Hamas takes over Gaza
2007	International conference to launch new peace process held in Annapolis, Maryland

OPERATION CAST LEAD THROUGH 2011

2008	Operation Cast Lead
2009	Israel agrees to ceasefire and withdraws troops from Gaza
2009	George Mitchell is named special envoy to the Middle East by President Barack Obama
2009	Benjamin Netanyahu becomes Israeli prime minister
2009	Pope Benedict XVI visits Israel
2009	Tel Aviv centennial celebrations held
2009	Israel agrees to ten-month settlement moratorium
2010	Peace talks with Palestinians begin and end
2011	"Arab Spring"
2011	Summer protests calling for social justice spread across Israel
2011	Light railway system opens in Jerusalem
2011	Turkey expels Israel's ambassador and downgrades ties
2011	Palestinians begin statehood push at the United Nations
2011	Quartet calls for new peace talks
2011	Gilad Shalit is released after five years; 1,027 Palestinian prisoners released
2011	Qaddafi killed during revolt in Libya
2011	Israel calls for a resumption of negotiations with Palestinians without preconditions

BIBLIOGRAPHY

Allon, Yigal. *The Making of Israel's Army*. Universe Books, 1970.

Amichai, Yehuda. *The Selected Poetry Of Yehuda Amichai, Newly Revised and Expanded edition*. University of California Press, 1996.

Aumann, Moshe. *Land Ownership in Palestine 1880-1948*. Academic Committee on the Middle East, 1976.

Avineri, Shlomo. *The Making of Modern Zionism: Intellectual Origins of the Jewish State*. Basic Books, 1981.

Avneri, Arieh. *The Claim of Dispossession*. Transaction Publishers, 1984.

Bard, Mitchell. *From Tragedy to Triumph: The Politics Behind the Rescue of Ethiopian Jewry*. Greenwood, 2002.

——. *Myths and Facts: A Guide to the Arab-Israeli Conflict*. AICE, 2011.

——. *The Water's Edge and Beyond*. Transaction Publishers, 1991.

——. *Will Israel Survive?* Palgrave, 2007.

Bard, Mitchell, and Moshe Schwartz. *1001 Facts Everyone Should Know About Israel*. Rowman & Littlefield, 2005.

Becker, Jillian. *The PLO*. St. Martin's Press, 1985.

Begin, Menachem. *The Revolt*. E. P. Dutton, 1978.

Bell, J. Bowyer. *Terror Out of Zion*. Transaction Publishers, 1996.

Ben-Ami, Yitshaq. *Years of Wrath, Days of Glory: Memoirs from the Irgun*. Shengold Publishers, 1996.

Ben-Gurion, David. *Rebirth and Destiny of Israel*. Philosophical Library, 1954.

Benvenisti, Meron. *City of Stone: The Hidden History of Jerusalem*. University of California Press, 1998.

Beverley, James A. *Understanding Islam*. Thomas Nelson, 2001.

Buehrig, Edward. *The UN and the Palestinian Refugees*. Indiana University Press, 1971.

Bush, George W. *Decision Points*. Crown, 2010.

Carter, Jimmy. *Keeping Faith: Memoirs of a President*. University of Arkansas Press, 1995.

Churchill, Randolph S., and Winston S. Churchill. *The Six-Day War*. Penguin, 1967.

Clinton, Bill. *My Life*. Vintage, 2005.

Cobban, Helena. *The Palestine Liberation Organization*. Cambridge University Press, 1984.

Collins, Larry, and Dominique Lapierre. *O Jerusalem!* Simon and Schuster, 1972.

Dimont, Max. *Jews, God and History*. Mentor Books, 1994.

Eban, Abba. *Heritage: Civilization and the Jews*. Summit Books, 1984.

———. *My Country: The Story of Modern Israel*. Random House, 1972.

Gilbert, Martin. *Israel: A History*. William Morrow & Co., 1998.

———. *Letters to Auntie Fori: The 5,000-Year History of the Jewish People and Their Faith*. Schocken, 2002.

Grossman, David. *Death as a Way of Life: From Oslo to the Geneva Agreement*. Picador, 2004.

———. *To the End of the Land*. Vintage, 2001.

———. *The Yellow Wind*. Picador, 2002.

Hertzberg, Arthur. *The Zionist Idea*. Jewish Publication Society, 1997.

Herzl, Theodor. *The Diaries of Theodor Herzl*. Peter Smith Publishers, 1987.

———. *The Jewish State*. Dover Publications, 1989.

Herzog, Chaim. *The Arab-Israeli Wars*. Random House, 1984.

———. *War of Atonement: The Inside Story of the Yom Kippur War*. Stackpole Books, 1998.

Hourani, Albert. *A History of the Arab Peoples*. Warner Books, 1992.

Israeli, Raphael, ed. *PLO in Lebanon*. St. Martin's Press, 1983.

Jabotinsky, Ze'ev. *The War and the Jew*. Altalena Press, 1987.

Johnson, Paul. *A History of the Jews*. HarperCollins, 1988.

Karsh, Efraim. *Fabricating Israeli History: The "New Historians."* Frank Cass, 2000.

——. *Palestine Betrayed*. Yale University Press, 2011.

Katz, Samuel. *Battleground: Fact and Fantasy in Palestine*. SPI Books, 1986.

Kissinger, Henry. *The White House Years*. Little Brown & Co., 1979.

——. *Years of Renewal*. Simon & Schuster, 1999.

Kollek, Teddy. *Jerusalem*. Washington Institute For Near East Policy, 1990.

Laqueur, Walter. *A History of Zionism*. Fine Communications, 1997.

——. *The Road to War*. Weidenfeld and Nicolson, 1968.

Laqueur, Walter, and Barry Rubin. *The Israel-Arab Reader*. Penguin, 2001.

Lewis, Bernard. *Islam and the West*. Oxford University Press, 1994.

——. *The Jews of Islam*. Princeton University Press, 2002.

——. *The Middle East: A Brief History of the Last 2000 Years*. Touchstone Books, 1997.

Livingstone, Neil C., and David Halevy. *Inside the PLO*. William Morrow and Co., 1990.

Lorch, Netanel. *One Long War*. Herzl Press, 1976.

Meir, Golda. *My Life*. Dell, 1975.

Morris, Benny. *The Birth of the Palestinian Refugee Problem Revisited*. Cambridge University Press, 2004.

——. *Righteous Victims: A History of the Zionist-Arab Conflict, 1881-1999*. Knopf, 2001.

Netanyahu, Benjamin. *A Place among the Nations: Israel and the World*. Warner Books, 1998.

Nixon, Richard. *RN: The Memoirs of Richard Nixon*. Touchstone Books, 1990.

O'Brien, Conner Cruise. *The Siege: The Saga of Israel and Zionism*. Touchstone Books, 1986.

Oren, Michael. *Six Days of War: June 1967 and the Making of the Modern Middle East*. Oxford University Press, 2002.

Oz, Amos. *In the Land of Israel*. Harvest Books. 1993.

——. *A Tale of Love and Darkness*. Harvest Books. 2005.

Patai, Ralph, ed. *Encyclopedia of Zionism and Israel*. McGraw Hill, 1971.

Porath, Yehoshua. *The Emergence of the Palestinian-Arab National Movement, 1918-1929*. Frank Cass, 1996.

——. *In Search of Arab Unity, 1930-1945*. Frank Cass, 1986.

——. *Palestinian Arab National Movement: From Riots to Rebellion: 1929-1939*. Vol. 2. Frank Cass, 1977.

Quandt, William B. *Camp David: Peacemaking and Politics*. Brookings Institution, 1986.

——, ed. *The Middle East: Ten Years after Camp David*. Brookings Institution, 1988.

Rabin, Yitzhak. *The Rabin Memoirs*. University of California Press, 1996.

Randal, Jonathan. *Going All the Way: Christian Warlords, Israeli Adventurers, and the War in Lebanon*. Vintage Books, 1983.

Reeve, Simon. *One Day in September: The Full Story of the 1972 Munich Olympics Massacre and the Israeli Revenge Operation "Wrath of God."* Arcade Publishing, 2001.

Ross, Dennis. *The Missing Peace: The Inside Story of the Fight for Middle East Peace*. Farrar, Straus and Giroux, 2004.

Roumani, Maurice. *The Case of the Jews from Arab Countries: A Neglected Issue*. World Organization of Jews from Arab Countries, 1977.

Rubinstein, Amnon. *The Zionist Dream Revisited: From Herzl to Gush Emunim and Back*. Schocken Books, 1987.

Sachar, Abram Leon. *History of the Jews*. Random House, 1982.

Sachar, Howard. *A History of Israel: From the Rise of Zionism to Our Time*. Alfred A. Knopf, 1998.

Safran, Nadav. *Israel: The Embattled Ally*. Harvard University Press, 1981.

Schechtman, Joseph B. *European Population Transfers, 1939-1945*. Russell & Russell, 1971.

Schiff, Ze'ev, and Ehud Ya'ari. *Intifada.* Simon & Schuster, 1990.

——. *Israel's Lebanon War.* Simon & Schuster, 1984.

Schoenberg, Harris. *Mandate for Terror: The United Nations and the PLO.* Shapolsky, 1989.

Silverberg, Robert. *If I Forget Thee O Jerusalem: American Jews and the State of Israel.* William Morrow and Co., Inc., 1970.

Stillman, Norman. *The Jews of Arab Lands.* Jewish Publication Society, 1989.

——. *The Jews of Arab Lands in Modern Times.* Jewish Publication Society, 1991.

Teveth, Shabtai. *Ben-Gurion and the Palestinian Arabs: From Peace to War.* Oxford University Press, 1985.

——. *Ben-Gurion: The Burning Ground 1886-1948.* Houghton Mifflin, 1987.

——. *Moshe Dayan: the Soldier, the Man, the Legend.* Houghton Mifflin, 1973.

Truman, Harry. *Years of Trial and Hope.* Vol. 2. Doubleday, 1956.

Weizmann, Chaim. *Trial and Error.* Greenwood Press, 1972.

Ye'or, Bat. *The Dhimmi.* Associated University Press, 1985.

WEBSITES

Academic Guide to Jewish History: www.library.utoronto.ca/jewishhistory

American Israel Public Affairs Committee (AIPAC): www.aipac.org

American Jewish Committee: www.ajc.org

Anti-Defamation League (ADL): www.adl.org

Arab-Islamic History: www.al-bab.com/arab/history.htm

Begin-Sadat Center for Strategic Studies: www.biu.ac.il/SOC/besa

Beit Hatfutsot—The Museum of the Jewish People: www.bh.org.il

Central Intelligence Agency (CIA): www.cia.gov

Central Zionist Archives: www.zionistarchives.org.il/ZA/pMainE.aspx

Dinur Center for the Study of Jewish History: www.dinur.org/resources

History of the Ancient Near East: ancientneareast.tripod.com

History of the Jewish People: www.jewishhistory.org.il

Institute for Advanced Strategic and Political Studies: www.israeleconomy.org/index.php

International Policy Institute for Counter-Terrorism: www.ict.org.il

Internet Medieval Sourcebook: www.fordham.edu/halsall/sbook.html

Internet Modern History Sourcebook:
   www.fordham.edu/halsall/mod/modsbook.html

Israel Defense Forces (IDF): www.idf.il

Israel Ministry of Foreign Affairs: www.mfa.gov.il

Israel's Central Bureau of Statistics: www.cbs.gov.il/engindex.htm

Israel's Prime Minister's Office: www.pmo.gov.il/PMOEng

Jerusalem Center for Public Affairs: www.jcpa.org

Jewish Institute for National Security Affairs (JINSA): www.jinsa.org

Jewish National Fund (JNF): www.jnf.org

Jewish Virtual Library: www.JewishVirtualLibrary.org

Knesset—The Israeli Parliament: www.knesset.gov.il

The Middle East Media Research Institute (MEMRI): www.memri.org

National Archives and Records Administration: www.archives.gov

Peres Center for Peace: www.peres-center.org

StandWithUs: www.standwithus.com

United Nations: www.un.org

U.S. Department of State: www.state.gov

Washington Institute for Near East Policy: www.washingtoninstitute.org

World Jewish Congress (WJC): www.worldjewishcongress.org

World Zionist Organization: www.en.wzo.org

 Use your smartphone to discover more Israel resources.

INDEX

ABOUT THE AUTHOR

Dr. Mitchell Bard is the executive director of the nonprofit American-Israeli Cooperative Enterprise (AICE), director of the Jewish Virtual Library, and a leading authority on US-Middle East policy. Dr. Bard is the author of numerous books, articles, and studies, and he has appeared on NBC, MSNBC, Fox News, CBC, al-Jazeera, and other local and national television and radio outlets.

He holds a doctorate in political science from the University of California, Los Angeles; a master's degree in public policy from the University of California, Berkeley; and a bachelor's degree in economics from the University of California, Santa Barbara.

Dr. Bard is also the author of *The Arab Lobby, 48 Hours of Kristallnacht, The Complete Idiot's Guide to Middle East Conflict, The Complete Idiot's Guide to World War II,* and *Myths and Facts: A Guide to the Arab-Israeli Conflict.*

For more information, visit his website at www.mitchellbard.com.

CREDITS

The author and publisher gratefully acknowledge the cooperation of the following sources of photographs and graphic images:

International Monetary Fund: 17; Israel Ministry of Foreign Affairs: 7, 22, 155; Israel Ministry of Tourism: insert page 1 (middle), insert page 1 (bottom), insert page 2 (bottom right), insert page 3 (bottom right), insert page 4 (bottom right), insert page 5 (top); Jewish Virtual Library: 57, 74, 89, 145; Library of Congress: 45; Shutterstock: Van Vugenfire cover (top), Dfree 13, Joao Virissimo 19, Joshua Haviv insert page 1 (top), Kobby Dagan insert page 2 (top left), Mikhail Levit insert page 2 (center left and bottom left), J van der Wolf insert page 2 (top right), Vadim Petrakov insert page 3 (top left), Kavrama insert page 3 (bottom left), Peter Zaharov insert page 3 (top right), Rostislav Ginsky insert page 4 (left), Voddol insert page 4 (top right), Gorshkov/25 insert page 5 (bottom); Stand With Us: 54 55, 65, 86, 98; Taglit-Birthright Israel: cover (bottom); Wiki/Creative Commons License: 11, 12, 42, 48, 52, 59, 61, 62, 71, 83, 95, 99, 108, 112, 126, 139, 140, 143, 160; World Economic Forum/Sharealike Commons License: 156; Ynhockey/Creative Commons License: 140

The graph on page 117 is based on statistics from the following sources: Israeli Central Bureau of Statistics; Jewish Telegraphic Agency; Jerusalem Post (August 8, 2001; February 3, 2003; August 17, 2006; October 29, 2010); Haaretz (August 27, 2005); YNET (January 4, 2006).